New Weight Watchers

Freestyle Cookbook #2019

Top Simple, Easy & Delicious Recipes to Lose Weight, Build Attractive Body & Upgrade Your Lifestyle

By

Andrea Zietlow

Copyright © **Andrea Zietlow** 2019

All rights reserved. No part of this publication maybe reproduced, stored or transmitted in any form or by any means, electronic, mechanical, photocopying, recording, scanning, or otherwise without written permission from the author. It is illegal to copy this book, post it to a website, or distribute it by any other means without permission.

Andrea Zietlow the moral right to be identified as the author of this work.

Table of Contents

Introduction 8

❖ WEIGHT WATCHERS BREAKFAST RECIPES ❖ 9

Breakfast Burritos (Weight Watchers) 9
Italian Baked Eggs (Weight Watchers) 10
Whole Wheat Apple Cinnamon Pancakes 11
Eggs Benedict 12
Apple Oatmeal Muffins 14
Broccoli Quiche 15
Cream Cheese Banana Stuffed French Toast 16
Peach Scones 17
Applesauce Cranberry Oatmeal 18
Crustless Spinach and Cheese Tarts 19
French Toast 20
Greek Scrambled Egg Wraps 21
Ham and Parmesan Cheese Omelet 23
Blueberry Streusel Muffins 24
Crustless Spinach and Mushroom Quiche 25
Slow Cooker Chocolate and Pistachio Oatmeal 26
Strawberry, Almond Butter, and Oatmeal Breakfast Parfait 27
Individual Egg & Spinach Bowls 28
Blueberry Chia Seed Pudding 29
Pita Pocket Breakfast Sandwich 30
Chocolate Oatmeal with Egg Whites 31
Wake Me Up, Keep Me Going Smoothie 32

Huevos Rancheros 33

Poppy Breakfast Muffins 34

Buckwheat Crepes with Fruit Filling and Yogurt 35

Protein Blueberry Quinoa Breakfast Bowl 36

Breakfast Berry & Yogurt Crunch.. 37

Overnight French Toast Casserole... 38

Protein Egg & Tomato Toast 39

Avocado & Egg Protein Wrap Recipe 40

❖ **WEIGHT WATCHERS LUNCH RECIPES** ❖ 41

Lemon-Pepper Tuna Sandwiches.. 41

Layered Mason Jar Quinoa and Veggie Salad 42

Chicken Salad with Walnuts and Grapes............................... 43

Chickpea and Spinach Stew 44

Fresh Mozzarella and Tomato Paninis 45

Grilled Ham and Cheese with Rosemary............................... 47

Turkey Taco Lettuce Wraps... 48

Mushroom and Steak Fajita Sandwiches................................ 49

Heirloom Tomato Salad 50

Wake Me Up, Keep Me Going Smoothie............................... 51

Asparagus Frittata with Herb Blossoms................................. 52

Crispy Mediterranean Vegetable Cakes 53

Tomato, Hummus, and Spinach Sandwich........................... 54

Baked Zucchini, Spinach, and Feta Casserole....................... 55

Meaty Veggie Roll-Ups 56

One Pot Turkey and Mediterranean Quinoa 57

Skinny Burrito in a Jar 58

Spring Mix with Roasted Pears and Feta 59

Old-Fashioned Vegetable Soup 60

Hearty Kale Salad 61

No-Mayo Chicken Salad 62

Mediterranean Tuna Salad 63

Slow Cooker Turkey Sloppy Joes 64

Supermodel Superfood Salad 65

Cucumber, Dill, and Cream Cheese Sandwiches 66

Thai Chicken Lettuce Cups 67

Tomatoes, Blueberries & Fennel Salad 68

Open Face Grilled Turkey Burgers 69

Monte Cristo Sandwiches 70

Tuna Salad 71

❖ **WEIGHT WATCHERS DINNER RECIPES** ❖ 72

Roasted Cauliflower Soup 72

Chicken and Black Bean Chili 73

Crock Pot Low-Fat Beef Stew 74

Farro & Cranberry Bean Soup 76

Slow Cooker Savory Superfood Soup 77

Slow Cooker Chicken Chili 78

Slow Cooker Turkey Stew 80

Slow Cooker Chicken Gyros 81

Zucchini Noodles Aglio et Olio 82

Grilled Turkey Veggie Burger 83

Mushroom and Steak Fajita Sandwiches 85

Turkey Taco Lettuce Wraps 86

Tomato, Hummus, and Spinach Sandwich 87

Skinny Tacos with Guacamole and Grilled Chicken 88

Slow Cooker Spinach Artichoke Chicken 89

Salmon with Ginger Noodles 90

Oven-Grilled Salmon 92

Slow Cooker Herb Chicken and Vegetables 92

Spicy Asian Chicken Meatballs 94

Mediterranean Tuna Salad 95

Southwestern Quinoa Salad 96

Fresh & Hearty Salad 97

Supermodel Superfood Salad 98

Kale and Roasted Yam Salad 99

Roast Butternut Squash and Chickpea Salad 100

6-Ingredient Mexican-Style Quinoa Salad 101

Avocado & Grape Salad with Walnuts 102

Creamy Fennel Salad, Orange Wedge, Fresh Mint 103

Lasagna with Fresh Tomatoes and Zucchini 105

Cauliflower Lasagna 106

❖ MORE HEALTHY WEIGHT WATCHER RECIPES ❖
.... 108

Asian Chicken and Veggie Lettuce Wraps 108

Slow Cooker Pork Tenderloin 109

Slow Cooker Brown Rice and Chicken 111

GRILLED SALMON & ASPARAGUS GRATED EGG, BALSAMIC DRESSING 113

German Schnitzel, Slow Cooker Style 114

Quinoa "Meatballs" | Vegetarian Meatball Recipe 116

Chicken Tikka Masala Pizza 118

Crustless Spinach Quiche with Sun-Dried Tomatoes 120

Slow Cooker Red Lentil Curry 122

Easy 20 Minute Chili 123

Conclusion 124

Introduction

There's no compelling reason to skip suppers when you're endeavoring to get in shape. Give yourself the best beginning to the day, with a solid and nutritious brekkie. Regardless of whether you're after a speedy in a hurried fix or an all-out cook, we have a lot of more beneficial options, without settling on taste.

Frequently our late morning dinner can finish up somewhat dreary, particularly in case we're on a wellbeing kick, yet we as a whole realize that winds up exhausting, no doubt! We have heaps of solid lunch thoughts, so you'll never be trapped in a hopeless cycle.

We have break time arranged whatever the event. Regardless of whether you're after supper for one, the family or a great spread for engaging, there are several formulas to look over. Also, you don't have to purchase extravagant fixings or slave over the stove for a considerable length of time!

❖ WEIGHT WATCHERS BREAKFAST RECIPES ❖

Breakfast Burritos (Weight Watchers)

Prep Time: 10mins, Cook Time: 20mins
Serving: 4, Smart Point: 9

Ingredients:

- 2 - tsp olive oil
- 2 - scallion, chopped
- 1 - green pepper, chopped
- 1 - tomato, chopped
- 2 - clove garlic, minced
- 2 - whole egg
- 4 - egg white
- ½ - cup low-fat cheddar cheese
- 2 - tbsp cilantro, chopped
- ¼ - tsp salt
- ¼ - tsp pepper
- 4 - whole wheat tortillas
- ½ - cup non-fat sour cream
- ½ - cup salsa

Instructions:

1. Preheat oven to 400 phases F. Oil a preparing dish with a nonstick cooking sprinkle.
2. Warmth olive oil in a skillet over medium warmth, by then, incorporates scallions, unpracticed pepper, tomato, and garlic and sauté for 5 minutes.
3. Blend in whole eggs and egg whites and after that cook till the eggs are needed doneness, cycle 3-5mins.
4. Oust from the glow and mix in cheddar, cilantro, salt, and pepper.
5. Recognize a tortilla on a plate and spoon in 1/4 of the filling, leave behind the burrito, and see it wrinkle angle down inside the prepared warming dish.
6. Get ready for 10mins and present with sharp cream and salsa.

Nutritional Information: Calories 298g, Fat 9g, Carbs 37g, Sugars 5g, Protein 17g

Italian Baked Eggs (Weight Watchers)

Prep Time: 10mins, Cook Time: 20mins
Serving: 4, Smart Point: 7

Ingredients:

- 2 - cup marinara sauce
- ¼ - cup fresh basil, chopped
- 4 - large egg
- ½ - cup parmesan cheese, grated
- ¼ - tsp red pepper flakes, or to taste, optional

Instructions:

1. Spot stove rack in the center position and preheat to 350 degrees F (175 degrees C).

2. Empty marinara sauce into a square heating dish or broiler verification skillet and sprinkle with basil.
3. Make 4 restricted wells and break an egg into the focal point of each. Sprinkle eggs with parmesan cheddar and red pepper chips.
4. Prepare for 18-20 minutes or until the egg whites are set and the yolks are wanted doneness.
5. Uniformly separate sauce among 4 singular dishes and spot an egg in each.

Nutritional Information: Calories 145.4g, Fat 2g, Carbs 16.6g, Sugars 4.1g, Protein 4.6g

Whole Wheat Apple Cinnamon Pancakes

Prep Time: 10mins, Cook Time: 10mins
Serving: 2, Smart Point: 5

Ingredients:

- ¾ - cup whole wheat flour
- ½ - tbsp baking powder
- 2 - tbsp artificial sweetener or sugar substitute, such as Splenda
- ½ - tbsp ground cinnamon
- 1 - cup skim milk or water
- 1 - whole egg white, lightly beaten
- 1/3 - cup unsweetened applesauce

Instructions:

1. In a bowl, consolidate entire wheat flour, preparing powder, sugar substitute, and cinnamon.
2. In a different bowl, combine skim milk or water, egg white, and fruit purée. Mix flour blend into egg blend until there are no irregularities.
3. Hitter will be thick, yet can be diminished to wanted consistency by including a tablespoon of water at once.

4. Warmth a vast skillet or frying pan and shower with a nonstick cooking splash.
5. Spoon two loading tablespoons of hitter per flapjack and spread out somewhat.
6. Cook until the hotcakes are brilliant dark colored on the two sides.

Nutritional Information: Calories 210g, Fat 1g, Carbs 43g, Sugars 0.3g, Protein 11g

Eggs Benedict

Prep Time: 20mins, Cook Time: 10mins
Serving: 4, Smart Point: 7

Ingredients:

- 1 - tbsp white wine or apple cider vinegar
- 4 - large egg, room temperature
- 4 - slice canadian bacon
- ¼ - cup fat free plain greek yogurt
- ¼ - cup reduced calorie mayonnaise
- 1 - tsp dijon mustard
- 1 - tsp lemon juice, freshly squeezed
- ½ - tsp lemon zest
- 2 - tsp unsalted butter, room temperature
- 2 - light whole grain English muffins, split and toasted

➢ 1 - medium tomato, cut into 4 thick slices

Instructions:

1. Top a huge skillet mostly off with water and heat to the point of boiling. Mix in vinegar, at that point diminishes warmth to a stew.
2. Cautiously break eggs each one in turn into the bubbling water. Cook for 4 minutes or until the whites is set.
3. Expel eggs with an opened spoon and let channel quickly. Put aside. Dispose of water.
4. Crash the skillet and set over medium-high warmth. Include Canadian bacon and cook for 1min each side or until warmed through.
5. To make the sauce: In a little microwave-safe bowl, whisk together, yogurt, mayonnaise, mustard, lemon juice, and lemon pizzazz.
6. Microwave for 30 seconds, at that point, blend in margarine until softened.
7. Spot a cut of tomato, Canadian bacon, and an egg on top every English biscuit half. Shower with around 2 tablespoons sauce.

Nutritional Information: Calories 92g, Fat 2.7g, Carbs 15.2g, Sugars 3.7g, Protein 4g

Apple Oatmeal Muffins

Prep Time: 10mins, Cook Time: 15mins
Serving: 12, Smart Point: 4

Ingredients:

- 2 - cup apple, peeled and shredded (about 2 small apples)
- 1 ½ - cup all-purpose flour
- 1 - cup quick cooking oats
- 2/3 - cup brown sugar, firmly packed
- 1 ½ - tsp baking powder
- ½ - tsp baking soda
- ½ - tsp salt
- ½ - tsp ground cinnamon
- ½ - cup milk
- 2 - tbsp vegetable oil

Instructions:

1. Preheat range to 375 degrees F (190 tiers C).
2. Splash 12 biscuit mugs with a nonstick cooking bathe or line with paper liners.
3. In a bowl, integrate flour, oats, dark-colored sugar, getting ready powder, heating tender drink, salt, cinnamon, milk, and vegetable oil till joined.
4. Equitably separate participant a number of the readied biscuit containers.
5. Heat for 15-18 minutes or till a toothpick embedded inside the focal factor of a biscuit confesses all.

Nutritional Information: Calories 167g, Fat 3g, Carbs 32g, Sugars 14g, Protein 3g

Broccoli Quiche

Prep Time: 10mins, Cook Time: 45mins
Serving: 6, Smart Point: 6

Ingredients:

- ¾ - cup liquid egg substitute
- 1 ½ - cup 1% low-fat milk
- ¾ - cup low-fat baking mix, such as Bisquick
- 1 - tsp salt
- ¼ - tsp black pepper, ground
- 2 - garlic cloves, chopped
- 20 - oz chopped frozen broccoli, or spinach
- 1 - medium onion, chopped
- 1 - red bell pepper, chopped
- 4 - oz part-skim mozzarella cheese

Instructions:

1. Defrost, flush, and channel broccoli.
2. Put 1/2 of broccoli in eleven x 7 glass skillet showered with cooking splash.
3. Put half onion, half ringer pepper and all of the cheddar further.
4. Put final broccoli, onion and ringer pepper similarly.
5. Mix egg substitute, milk, bread combo, salt, dark pepper, and garlic in a blender till easy.
6. Pour combo over broccoli in skillet.
7. Heat at four hundred tiers for 50 minutes or until softly caramelized.
8. Cut into 6 portions when cool.

Nutritional Information: Calories 114g, Fat 4g, Carbs 11g, Sugars 6g, Protein 10g

Cream Cheese Banana Stuffed French Toast

Prep Time: 15mins, Cook Time: 10mins
Serving: 2, Smart Point: 10

Ingredients:

- 4 - piece bread, 3/8 inch thick
- 2 - tbsp neufchatel or light cream cheese
- 1 - medium sized ripe banana
- ¼ - cup low-fat milk
- 1 - large egg
- ¼ - tsp vanilla extract
- 1 - tsp unsalted butter
- 2 - tbsp maple syrup, warmed
- 6 - fresh strawberries, sliced, for garnish, optional

Instructions:

1. Spread Neufchatel or light cream cheddar on each of the 4 bits of bread.
2. Spot banana cuts on 2 bits of the bread and best each with residual bread.
3. In a little shallow bowl, beat together milk, egg, and vanilla concentrate.
4. Dissolve margarine in an extensive nonstick skillet over medium warmth.

5. Quickly plunge sandwiches, each one in turn, into the egg blend.
6. Spot the two sandwiches in the skillet and cook until brilliant dark colored, 3-4 minutes on each side. Present with maple syrup and strawberries, whenever wanted.

Nutritional Information: Calories 362g, Fat 10g, Carbs 59g, Sugars 26g, Protein 11g

Peach Scones

Prep Time: 15mins, Cook Time: 14mins
Serving: 4, Smart Point: 4

Ingredients:

- 2/3 - cup all-purpose flour
- 2 - tbsp sugar
- ½ - tsp baking powder
- ¼ - tsp baking soda
- 1 - dash salt
- 1 - tbsp chilled butter or margarine, cut into small pieces
- 1/3 - cup low-fat vanilla yogurt
- 2 - tbsp dried peach, chopped
- 1 - cooking spray
- ½ - tsp non-fat milk
- 1 - tsp sugar

Instructions:

1. Preheat broiler to 400 degrees Fahrenheit.
2. Join flour, sugar, preparing powder, heating soft drink, and salt in a bowl.
3. Cut in margarine with a cake blender or 2 blades until blend takes after coarse supper.
4. Add yogurt and dried peaches to flour blend, mixing just until damp.

5. Turn batter out onto a gently floured surface, and massage daintily 4 or multiple times; mixture might be marginally sticky.
6. Pat batter into a 5-inch hover on a heating sheet covered with cooking shower.
7. Cut hover into 4 wedges; separate wedges somewhat.
8. Brush milk over batter and sprinkle with 1 teaspoon sugar.
9. Prepare for 14 minutes or until brilliant.

Nutritional Information: Calories 159g, Fat 3g, Carbs 29g, Sugars 10g, Protein 3g

Applesauce Cranberry Oatmeal

Prep Time: 2mins, Cook Time: 2mins
Serving: 1, Smart Point: 3

Ingredients:

- 3 - tbsp uncooked oatmeal
- 1 - tbsp dried cranberry
- ½ - cup unsweetened applesauce
- ½ - cup water
- 1/8 - tsp ground cinnamon

Instructions:

1. Blend cereal, cranberries, fruit purée, water, and cinnamon together.
2. Microwave for 1-2 minutes.

Nutritional Information: Calories 111g, Fat 1g, Carbs 25g, Sugars 12g, Protein 2g

Crustless Spinach and Cheese Tarts

Prep Time: 15mins, Cook Time: 30mins
Serving: 12, Smart Point: 3

Ingredients:

- 1 - cup onion, hopped
- 1 - tsp garlic, minced
- 1 - cup roasted red pepper
- 5 - oz fresh baby spinach
- 2 - large egg
- 1 - cup low-fat milk
- 1 - cup reduced-fat baking mix
- 1 - cup reduced-fat mozzarella cheese
- 2 - tbsp fresh basil leaves
- ½ - tsp salt
- ¼ - tsp black pepper
- ¼ - cup parmesan cheese

Instructions:

1. Preheat stove to four hundred degrees F (205 levels C). Shower a customary size 12 container biscuit dish with a nonstick cooking splash.
2. Splash an expansive nonstick skillet with nonstick cooking bathe and notice over medium-excessive warmth.
3. Include onion and sauté; blending usually, for eight to 10 minutes or till the onion is translucent.
4. Include garlic, pink peppers, and spinach and prepare dinner, blending regularly, for 1 to 2mins or till the spinach is gotten smaller.

5. Whisk together eggs and milk in a sizable bowl. Blend in cooked greens, heating mixture, mozzarella cheddar, basil, salt, and darkish pepper.
6. Equitably isolate mixture many of the readied biscuit mugs, round 1/3 glass every.
7. Heat for 15 minutes or till the truffles are actually set. Expel from the stove and sprinkle each with 1 teaspoon parmesan cheddar.
8. Come returned to the broiler and put together for five extra minutes or until the cakes are softly sautéed and cooked thru.

Nutritional Information: Calories 196.5g, Fat 12.7g, Carbs 10.9g, Sugars 1.6g, Protein 9.5g

French Toast

Prep Time: 5mins, Cook Time: 5mins
Serving: 2, Smart Point: 3

Ingredients:

- 4 - egg white
- ¼ - cup skim milk
- 1 - tbsp vanilla extract
- 1 - butter flavored cooking spray
- 6 - slice reduced calorie wheat bread
- 1 - tbsp ground cinnamon
- 1 - sugar free maple syrup

Instructions:

1. Whisk collectively egg whites, milk, and vanilla concentrate in a shallow bowl.
2. Shower a huge nonstick skillet with cooking splash and heat over medium warmth.
3. Working in bunches, dunk each cut of bread inside the egg mixture for 30 seconds on every side.

4. Give a part of the player a hazard to trickle off, at that point region in the skillet.
5. Cook for two-3mins on each facet till wonderful darkish colored. Exchange to a plate and maintain heat.
6. Shower the skillet with a cooking splash if crucial and rehash with residual bread.
7. A residue with cinnamon and gift with syrup.

Nutritional Information: Calories 50g, Fat 0.3g, Carbs 4g, Sugars 1g, Protein 6g

Greek Scrambled Egg Wraps

Prep Time: 10mins, Cook Time: 10mins
Serving: 2, Smart Point: 13

Ingredients:

- 1 - low-fat cooking spray
- ½ - red onion
- 1 - small zucchini
- 8 - cherry tomato
- ¼ - cup black olives
- ½ - cup reduced-fat feta cheese
- 4 - egg
- 1 ½ - tsp greek seasoning
- 4 to 6 - flour tortilla

Instructions:

1. Splash a non-stick skillet with a touch of the cooking shower.
2. Finely dice the red onion and put aside.
3. Shred/grind the zucchini and lay the tissue on a paper towel to splash up any dampness.

4. Quarter the cherry tomatoes, rub out the seeds and finely dice the substance.
5. Lay the tissue on a paper towel additionally to douse up any dampness.
6. Finely slash the dark olives and the feta cheddar. Put both aside, independently.
7. Beat the eggs with the Greek flavoring.
8. Sauté the hacked onion in the non-stick skillet for 2 minutes over medium warmth, blending.
9. Include the zucchini, tomatoes, and olives and cook for a further moment.
10. Include the beaten eggs cook, as yet blending, for 3-4 minutes or until done.
11. On each wrap, place a portion of the egg blend and best it with feta cheddar. Overlap over the wrap and appreciate.

Nutritional Information: Calories 383g, Fat 16g, Carbs 40g, Sugars 6g, Protein 19g

Ham and Parmesan Cheese Omelet

Prep Time: 10mins, Cook Time: 6mins
Serving: 2, Smart Point: 5

Ingredients:

- 2 - Whole large egg
- 4 - large egg white
- 2 - tbsp green onion, chopped
- ¼ - tsp salt
- 1/8 - tsp black pepper
- 1/8 - tsp hot pepper sauce, or to taste
- ½ - cup cooked lean ham, diced
- ¼ - cup parmesan cheese

Instructions:

1. Whisk collectively eggs, egg whites, green onion, salt, dark pepper, and hot sauce in a big bowl.
2. Shower a nonstick skillet with cooking splash and notice it over medium warmth.
3. Pour within the egg combination, and in a while tilting the skillet so the bottom is definitely secured.
4. Infrequently raise the cooked egg, so any uncooked egg can flow to the rims of the skillet.
5. Sprinkle with ham and parmesan cheddar.

6. Relax the edges of the omelet and tenderly overlay it into same components.
7. Cook for 1 progressively second or till warmed via.

Nutritional Information: Calories 1224g, Fat 80g, Carbs 85g, Sugars 4g, Protein 45g

Blueberry Streusel Muffins

Prep Time: 20mins, Cook Time: 35mins
Serving: 12, Smart Point: 6

Ingredients:

- 2 ¼ - cup all-purpose flour, divided
- 1 - tsp baking powder
- ½ - tsp baking soda
- ½ - tsp salt
- 1 - cup white sugar, divided
- 2 - tbsp butter, melted
- 1 - large egg
- ¾ - cup reduced-fat sour cream
- 1 - tsp vanilla extract
- ¼ - cup fat free skim milk, divided
- 2 - cup fresh blueberries

Instructions:

1. Preheat broiler to 375 ranges F (one hundred ninety ranges C). Line a 12 glass biscuit field with paper liners.
2. In a tremendous bowl, be part of 2 mugs flour, getting ready powder, heating soft drink, and salt and placed apart.
3. To make the streusel topping: In a touch bowl, consolidate closing 1/4 glass flour and 1/four field sugar.
4. Pour in the liquefied unfold and join until the mixture is brittle.

5. In a huge bowl, beat egg with exquisite 3/four glass sugar till mild and fleecy.
6. Include harsh cream and beat until altogether joined. Blend in vanilla listen.
7. Then once more blend in 1/2 of the dry fixings and half of the milk until in reality consolidated. Overlay in blueberries.
8. Fill each biscuit glass around 3/4 complete. Uniformly sprinkle streusel beating over each over biscuit.
9. Cool within the searches for gold to 15mins, at that factor trade biscuits to wire racks to chill absolutely.

Nutritional Information: Calories 360g, Fat 11g, Carbs 59g, Sugar 33g, Protein 7g

Crustless Spinach and Mushroom Quiche

Prep Time: 5mins, Cook Time: 60mins
Serving: 4, Smart Point: 3

Ingredients:

- 10 - oz frozen spinach
- 1 - cup mushrooms, sliced
- 1 - cup artichoke hearts, chopped
- ½ - tsp olive oil
- ½ - cup fat-free cottage cheese
- 2 - tsp garlic, minced
- ½ - medium onion, chopped
- 3 - egg
- 1 - salt
- 1 - black pepper
- 1 - nonstick cooking spray

Instructions:

1. Preheat stove to 350 degrees.
2. Sauté mushrooms and onions in olive oil with garlic.

3. Include spinach and cook until the fluid has diminished.
4. Blend vegetables with residual fixings, salt, and pepper to taste.
5. Fill pie dish splashed with nonstick shower. Prepare 45 minutes.

Nutritional Information: Calories 128g, Fat 5g, Carbs 12g, Sugars 2g, Protein 11g

Slow Cooker Chocolate and Pistachio Oatmeal

Prep Time: 25mins, Cooking Time: 45mins
Serving: 4, Smart Point: 8

Ingredients:

- Oil for coating the slow cooker
- 1 - cup steel-cut oats
- 5 - cups water
- 2 - tablespoons cocoa powder
- 4 - tablespoons crushed pistachios
- 2 - tablespoons coconut sugar

Instructions:

1. Coat the base of the moderate cooker with a little measure of any unbiased seasoned sound oil like almond oil, safflower oil, and so on.
2. In the moderate cooker, consolidate the oats, water, cocoa powder, half of the pistachios, and sugar.
3. Set the moderate cooker on low for 1-1/2 hours at that point abandon it to keep warm naturally while you are resting.
4. Mix it in the first part of the day at that point sprinkle the rest of the pistachios and include some low-fat milk on the off chance that you want.

Nutrition Information: Calories 254g, Fat 12g, Carbs 30g, Sugars 1g, Protein 9g

Strawberry, Almond Butter, and Oatmeal Breakfast Parfait

Prep Time: 10mins, Cooking Time: 20mins
Serving: 2, Smart Point: 4

Ingredients:

- ½ - cup rolled oats
- 1 - cup water
- ¼ - cup almond milk
- 1 - teaspoon vanilla
- 1 - tablespoon almond butter
- 2 - frozen bananas
- 1 - cup sliced strawberries
- Sliced almonds and strawberries

Instructions:

1. Join the oats and water in a pan and cook over low warmth for 5-6 minutes.

2. Blend in the almond milk, vanilla, and almond spread. Blend until almond spread is liquefied.
3. Turn off warmth and permit to cool somewhat.
4. At the point when the oats are somewhat warm, however not hot, put the bananas and strawberries in a blender.
5. Mix, driving fixings down with an alter if fundamental.
6. Include a tablespoon or two of almond milk to help mix if vital, being mindful so as not to include excessively
7. To serve, layer the warm oats with the solidified strawberry blend in a container or parfait glass.
8. Top with cut almonds and strawberries and eat with a spoon.

Nutrition Information: Calories 263g, Fat 7g, Carbs 48g, Sugars 19g, Protein 6g

Individual Egg & Spinach Bowls

Time: Prep Time: 15mins, Cooking Time: 25mins
Serving: 4, Smart Point: 1

Ingredients:

- 8 - large egg whites
- 1 - whole egg
- 1 - cup baby spinach
- ½ - cup diced tomatoes
- ¼ - cup feta cheese
- ½ - teaspoon black pepper
- Kosher or sea salt

Instructions:

1. Preheat broiler to 350 degrees.
2. Whisk together all fixings in a medium blending bowl. Softly fog 4 ramekins with nonstick cooking shower and equally partition egg blend into dishes.

3. Spot ramekins on a treated sheet and prepare 20 minutes or until eggs puff and are nearly set in the inside. Serve hot.

Nutrition Information: Calories 84g, Fat 2g, Carbs 6g, Sugars 2g, Protein 11g

Blueberry Chia Seed Pudding

Prep Time: 35mins, Cooking Time: 40mins
Serving: 4, Smart Point: 7

Ingredients:

- 1 ½ - cups almond milk
- ½ - cup chia seeds
- 2 - tablespoons honey
- ½ - teaspoon vanilla extract
- 1 - cup blueberries
- ¼ - cup granola for topping

Instructions:

1. Join the milk, nectar, vanilla, and blueberries in a blender until pureed. Speed in the chia seeds.
2. Fill singular bricklayer containers, ramekins or glasses.

3. Spread and spot in the refrigerator for no less than 3 to 5 hours and up to medium-term, or until a thick, pudding-like consistency is accomplished.

Nutrition Information: Calories 172g, Fat 6g, Carbs 26g, Sugars 17g, Protein 4g

Pita Pocket Breakfast Sandwich

Prep Time: 20mins, Cooking Time: 25mins
Serving: 2, Smart Point: 6

Ingredients:

- 2 - large eggs
- 2 - large egg whites
- 1 - tablespoon milk
- 1 - cup baby spinach torn into small pieces
- 4 - grape tomatoes sliced in half lengthwise
- 2 - green onions, diced
- Sea salt and pepper to taste
- ¼ - cup Feta cheese crumbles
- 1 - whole wheat pita pocket
- 2 - teaspoons olive oil

Instructions:

1. Preheat stove to 350 degrees.
2. In a medium combining bowl whisk eggs, egg whites, milk, spinach, tomatoes, green onions, and salt and pepper to taste.
3. Empty egg blend into an 8" non-stick skillet, place in the stove on center rack.
4. Brush the two sides of every pita half with olive oil, place on foil and warm in the broiler amid the most recent 2 minutes of cooking time.
5. Cook eggs roughly 15 to 18 minutes or until puffy and simply set in the inside, yet not hard.

6. Sprinkle on the feta cheddar and come back to the stove for one progressively minute.
7. Expel skillet from broiler, cut omelet down the middle and spot every half in a pita stash.
8. Press edges into a warm pita and serves right away.

Nutrition Information: Calories 297g, Fat 12g, Carbs 21g, Sugars 2g, Protein 21g

Chocolate Oatmeal with Egg Whites

Prep Time: 10mins, Cooking Time: 15mins
Serving: 1, Smart Point: 7

Ingredients:

- 1 - cup water
- 1/3 - cup rolled oats
- 1 - tablespoon chia seeds
- 1 - tablespoon cocoa powder
- ½ - teaspoon cinnamon
- ½ - ripe banana
- ¼ - cup pumpkin puree
- ¼ - teaspoon vanilla extract
- ¼ - cup egg whites

Instructions:

1. Heat water to the point of boiling. Blend in oats, chia seeds, cocoa, and cinnamon and lower heat.
2. Include banana. Cook ~5 minutes. Blend intermittently, separating banana pieces.
3. Include pumpkin when water is about 75% ingested.
4. Mix indelicately. Cook an additional couple of minutes.
5. At the point when water is practically all ingested, including the vanilla.
6. Include egg whites and whisk 2-3 minutes until they have liquefied in.

7. Spread pot with a top for ~5 minutes.
8. Top with wanted garnishes and appreciate.

Nutrition Information: Calories 197g, Fat 5.2g, Carbs 37.9g, Sugars 7.6g, Protein 6.7g

Wake Me Up, Keep Me Going Smoothie

Prep Time: 5mins, Cooking Time: 15mins
Serving: 2, Smart Point: 8

Ingredients:

- 1 - frozen banana
- ½ - cup frozen grapes of any color
- ½ - avocado
- 1 - cup spinach
- 1 - cup kale, removes stem and discard
- 2 - tablespoons chia seeds
- 1 ½ - cups chilled green tea, unsweetened
- Ice if needed

Instructions:

1. Add all fixings to the blender, with the exception of ice, mix until smooth.
2. Include ice for a thicker smoothie.
3. Suggest natural or homegrown spinach and kale.

Nutrition Information: Calories 245g, Fat 4.2g, Carbs 46.8g, Sugars 20.1g, Protein 8.1g

Huevos Rancheros

Prep Time: 5mins, Cooking Time: 15mins
Serving: 4, Smart Point: 12

Ingredients:

- 15 - ounce black beans
- 1 - teaspoon cumin
- ½ - teaspoon kosher or sea salt
- ½ - teaspoon black pepper
- 1 - tablespoon extra-virgin olive oil
- 4 - large eggs
- 1 - avocado
- 1 - tomato, chopped
- ½ - cup crumbled feta cheese
- ½ - cup chopped cilantro

Instructions:

1. In a skillet, include dark beans, cumin, 1/4 teaspoon salt, 1/4 teaspoon pepper, and half tablespoon extra virgin olive oil.
2. Cook over medium warm temperature for around five minutes.
3. Make 4 areas between beans. Include ultimate 1/2 olive oil to every area.
4. Break an egg into each area, decrease warmth, and allow cooking for around five minutes.
5. Expel from the warm temperature and sprinkle eggs with staying salt and pepper.
6. Include cheddar disintegrates, avocado portions, tomatoes, and sprinkle with hacked cilantro.
7. Present with salsa, on every occasion desired.

Nutrition Information: Calories 327.3, Fat 8.2g, Carbs 37.3g, Sugars 1.2g, Protein 26.3g

Poppy Breakfast Muffins

Prep Time: 15mins, Cooking Time: 45mins
Serving: 12, Smart Point: 9

Ingredients:

Wet Ingredients:

- 1 - cup uncooked quinoa
- ¾ - cup milk of any variety
- 2/3 - cup honey
- ¼ - cup olive oil
- 1 - large egg
- 1-½ - teaspoons almond extract

Dry Ingredients:

- 2 - cups white whole wheat flour
- 1-½ - teaspoons baking powder
- ¼ - teaspoon kosher or sea salt
- ½ - teaspoon baking soda
- 1/3 - cup poppy seeds

Instructions:

1. Preheat stove to 350 degrees. Line a biscuit tin with papers or oil with a light layer of the cooking shower.
2. Heat quinoa to the point of boiling in 1-2/3 container water.
3. Lessen warmth to the most reduced setting, spread, and cook for 20 minutes until all water is assimilated. Lighten with a fork.
4. Whisk together the majority of the dry fixings.
5. In a different bowl, whisk together the majority of the wet fixings and afterward add to the dry fixings.

6. Overlay wet blend into dry blend until simply joined.
7. Fill every biscuit tin and heat for around 25 minutes or until a toothpick embedded in the inside tells the truth.
8. Appreciate

Nutrition Information: Calories 254g, Fat 8g, Carbs 41g, Sugar 17g, Protein 6g

Buckwheat Crepes with Fruit Filling and Yogurt

Prep Time: 25mins, Cooking Time: 45mins
Serving: 8, Smart Point: 11

Ingredients:

- 5 - tablespoons coconut oil
- 2/3 - cup buckwheat flour
- 1/3 - cup white whole wheat flour
- 3 - large eggs
- 1 - cup low-fat plain Greek yogurt
- 1 - tablespoon honey
- 1 - teaspoon vanilla
- 3 - kiwis
- 1 - mango or peach
- 1 - banana

Instructions:

1. Cleave foods are grown from the ground yogurt with nectar and vanilla.
2. Include coconut oil, the two flours, and eggs in a blender or nourishment processor and mix until completely consolidated.
3. Include one teaspoon of coconut oil in an 8-inch nonstick skillet over medium warmth.
4. Include 1/3 glass scoop of hitter and twirl with the back of the spoon to frame a level crepe.
5. Cook for 2 minutes, extricates the edges with a spatula and cook for an extra 30 seconds until cooked through.
6. Spread and rehash with whatever is left of the blend.
7. Serve crepes warm with the new organic product inside and a touch of yogurt in each.
8. Appreciate

Nutrition Information: Calories 246g, Fat 13g, Carbs 28g, Sugar 14g, Protein 8g

Protein Blueberry Quinoa Breakfast Bowl

Prep Time: 15mins, Cooking Time: 35mins
Serving: 4, Smart Point: 7

Ingredients:

- 1 - cup uncooked quinoa, pre-rinsed
- 2 - cups fat-free milk
- 2 - tablespoons honey
- 1 - cup fresh blueberries
- Zest of 1 lemon
- Red currants or Goji berries

Instructions:

1. Over medium warmth, in a medium pot, heat quinoa and milk to the point of boiling.
2. Spread and diminish warmth to a stew. Cook the quinoa until milk is retained, roughly 15 minutes.
3. Include the nectar, blueberries, and lemon get-up-and-go, mix to join. Serve in individual dishes.
4. Whenever wanted, embellish with organic product improved jam.

Nutrition Information: Calories 243g, Fat 3g, Carbs 44g, Sugars 8g, Protein 11g

Breakfast Berry & Yogurt Crunch

Prep Time: 10mins, Cooking Time: 35mins
Serving: 2, Smart Point: 12

Ingredients:

- 1 - cup plain Greek yogurt
- 2 - tablespoons raw honey
- ½ - teaspoon vanilla extract
- 2/3 - cup clean eating granola
- 1 - cup fresh berries

Instructions:

1. Whisk together yogurt, nectar, and vanilla in a bowl.
2. In two slight containers or parfait glasses, layer multiple times in a specific order: granola, berries, and yogurt blend.
3. Spare a couple of berries for adding to the best.
4. Appreciate

Nutrition Information: Calories 296g, Fat 2g, Carbs 56g, Sugar 38g, Protein 18g

Overnight French Toast Casserole

Prep Time: 15mins, Cooking Time: 45mins
Serving: 10, Smart Point: 6

Ingredients:

- 13 - ounce loaf whole wheat French bread
- 8 - large eggs
- 2 - cups low-fat milk
- 1 - teaspoon pure vanilla extract
- 1 - teaspoon cinnamon
- 2 - tablespoons coconut palm sugar

Topping:

- ¼ - cup sucanat
- ½ - cup minced pecans
- 1 - teaspoon cinnamon

Instructions:

1. Softly for a 9" x 13" x 2" meal dish with non-stick cooking shower.
2. Organize bread cuts in two columns, somewhat covering pieces. In a huge blending bowl, whisk together eggs, milk, vanilla, cinnamon, and sucanat.
3. Pour blend over bread, ensuring all bread is wet. Spread and refrigerate medium-term.

4. Preheat broiler to 350 degrees. Consolidate topping fixings, sprinkle equitably absurd of bread and heat 35 to 40 minutes, or until brilliant.
5. Present with new berries or a shower of unadulterated maple syrup.

Nutrition Information: Calories 299g, Fat 2g, Carbs 38g, Sugars 14g, Protein 15g

Protein Egg & Tomato Toast

Prep Time: 5mins, Cooking Time: 15mins
Serving: 4, Smart Point: 5

Ingredients:

- 4 - large eggs
- 1 - teaspoon lemon juice
- 2 - Roma tomatoes
- 4 - leaves iceberg
- 4 - slices whole grain
- ½ - teaspoon salt
- ½ - teaspoon black pepper

Instructions:

1. Include 2-creeps of water in a field with the lemon juice or vinegar and half of the salt and bring to a stew over high warm temperature.
2. Split an egg into a little bowl or mug and afterward slide the egg into the water.
3. On the off threat that water progresses toward becoming too hot, lessen the temperature to maintain at a stew.
4. Cook for around 3 to four minutes till the whites are company but the yolks are nonetheless liquefied.
5. Evacuate eggs with an opened spoon and notice on a plate.
6. Include one poached egg, lettuce, and tomato to each toast cut.

7. Season with salt and pepper.

Nutrition Information: Calories 154g, Fat 6g, Carbs 15g, Sugars 3g, Protein 10g

Avocado & Egg Protein Wrap Recipe

Prep Time: 15mins, Cooking Time: 20mins
Serving: 4, Smart Point: 10

Ingredients:

- 6 - inch whole grain tortillas
- 4 - eggs
- 2 - avocados, peeled and seed removed
- 3 - teaspoons extra-virgin olive oil
- 2 - teaspoons balsamic vinegar
- ¼ - teaspoon kosher or sea salt
- ¼ - teaspoon black pepper

Instructions:

1. Preheat stove to 350 ranges.
2. Stack tortillas and enclose by foil. Warmth within the broiler for 10 minutes.
3. Wrap tortillas in marginally clammy paper towels and microwave for 30 seconds.
4. Consolidate avocado, 1 teaspoon olive oil, and vinegar in a bowl. Put aside.
5. In a huge nonstick skillet over medium-low warm temperature, encompass 2 teaspoons olive oil and warmth simply until warm, but now not smoking.
6. Delicately encompass eggs, everyone in flip, taking attention no longer to interrupt the yolks.
7. Cook simply till whites are set and yolks are marginally thickened.
8. Meanwhile, uniformly bring mixture over warmed tortillas. Spot eggs over avocado blend.

9. Sprinkle with salt and pepper. Fold into a wrap, whenever wanted.

Nutrition Information: Calories 317g, Fat 24g, Carbs 20g, Sugars 1g, Protein 10g

❖ WEIGHT WATCHERS LUNCH RECIPES ❖

Lemon-Pepper Tuna Sandwiches

Prep Time: 15mins, Cooking Time: 5mins
Serving: 2, Smart Point: 17

Ingredients:

- 6- oz water-packed tuna fish drained
- ½ small uncooked carrots
- 2 Tbsp reduced calorie mayonnaise
- 2 Tbsp fresh parsley
- 1 medium uncooked shallots
- 1 Tb8p fresh lemon juice
- 1 tsp lemon zest
- ½ tsp black pepper
- 4 slice reduced calorie wheat bread
- ½ cups arugula

Instructions

1. Consolidate all fixings, with the exception of bread and arugula, in a little bowl; blend well.
2. Layer 2 cuts toast with 1/4 container arugula and around 1/2 glass fish plate of mixed greens; top with outstanding cuts toast and serve.

Nutrition Information: Calories 373g, Fat 21.7g, Carbs 36.8g, Sugar 5.1g, Protein 11.9g

Layered Mason Jar Quinoa and Veggie Salad

Prep Time: 22mins, Cooking Time: 15mins
Serving: 8, Smart Point: 23

Ingredients:

- 1 cups uncooked quinoa
- ¾ pounds uncooked string beans
- 2 Tbsp dill fresh, chopped
- 2 medium corn kernels cut off cob
- 1 small jalapeño peppers
- 1 cups sweet red peppers
- 1 medium nectarines
- 1 ½ tsp lemon zest
- 1 ½ Tbsp fresh lemon juice
- 4 Tbsp canola oil
- 1 Tbsp Dijon Mustard
- ¼ tsp Sugar
- ½ tsp kosher salt
- 1 pinch black pepper

Instructions:

1. Cook quinoa as indicated by bundle directions; lighten with a fork and let cool to room temperature.

2. Whiten green beans in salted water; channel and hurl with dill.
3. Hurl corn with jalapeno.
4. Uniformly partition and layer corn, quinoa, red pepper, green beans and nectarine among 8 slight artisan containers screw cover on and refrigerate until prepared to serve.
5. Whisk together lemon pizzazz and juice, oil, mustard, sugar, salt and pepper in a bowl.
6. At the point when prepared to serve, spoon 1 Tbsp dressing into each container and shake to coat equitably.

Nutrition Information: Calories 471g, Fat 33.6g, Carbs 20.4g, Sugar 11.9g, Protein24.2g

Chicken Salad with Walnuts and Grapes

Prep time: 20mins, Cooking time: 5mins
Serving: 4, Smart Point: 9

Ingredients:

- ¼ cups Plain fat free yogurt
- ¼ cups fat free mayonnaise
- ¼ tsp ginger root
- 6 oz roasted skinless boneless chicken breast
- 2 medium uncooked scallions
- ¼ cups grapes
- ¼ cups uncooked celery
- ¼ cups uncooked carrots
- 2 Tbsp chopped walnuts

Instructions:

1. In a huge bowl, consolidate yogurt, mayonnaise, and ginger; include chicken and mix until chicken is all around covered.

2. Include scallions, grapes, celery, carrots, and walnuts; tenderly mix, spread and chill until prepared to serve.

Nutrition Information: Calories 242.8g, Fat 6.6g, Carbs 38.4g, Sugars 3g, Protein 8.4g

Chickpea and Spinach Stew

Prep Time: 16mins, Cooking Time: 22mins
Serving: 6, Smart Point: 7

Ingredients:

- 2 tsp olive oil
- 2 small uncooked onions
- 1 tsp table salt
- 2 medium cloves garlic clove(s)
- 2 tsp ground cumin
- 1 tsp ground ginger
- 15 oz canned diced tomatoes
- 3 cans chickpeas
- 10 oz fresh spinach
- 2 Tbsp water
- 1 Tbsp fresh lemon juice

- ¼ cups cilantro

Instructions:

1. Warmth oil in a substantial nonstick skillet over medium-low warmth.
2. Include onion and 1/2 teaspoon salt; cook, mixing as often as possible, until relaxed, around 10 minutes. Mix in garlic, cumin, and ginger; cook for 1 minute.
3. Include tomatoes and their juice, and chickpeas; blend to join and squash chickpeas somewhat with a potato masher.
4. Utilizing tongs, hurl in spinach and sprinkle blend with water; cook, secured, until spinach is withered, hurling blend once part of the way through, around 5 to 10 minutes. Blend in lemon juice, cilantro and remaining 1/2 teaspoon salt. Yields around 1/4 containers for every serving.

Nutrition Information: Calories 227.2g, Fat 9g, Carbs 8.8g, Sugars 0.5g, Protein 27.6g

Fresh Mozzarella and Tomato Paninis

Prep time: 10mins, Cooking Time: 4mins
Serving: 4, Smart Point: 13

Ingredients:

- 1 ½ tsp red wine vinegar
- ½ tsp olive oil
- ¼ tsp dried oregano
- ⅛ tsp table salt
- ⅛ tsp black pepper
- 4 oz Italian bread
- 2 oz whole milk mozzarella cheese
- 1 cups arugula
- 1 medium plum tomatoes

- ➢ 4 sprays olive oil cooking spray
- ➢ 1 medium cloves garlic cloves

Instructions:

1. Preheat open-air barbecue.
2. In a little glass, mix together vinegar, oil, oregano, salt, and pepper until mixed. Brush blend onto 1 side of each cut of bread.
3. To make each sandwich, layer 1/4 of cheddar over the brushed side of bread and after that top with 2 tomato cuts and 1/4 measure of arugula.
4. Top with another cut of bread brushed side down and after that coat sandwiches with a cooking splash.
5. Rehash with outstanding fixings.
6. Flame broil, gently squeezing with a spatula every now and then, until bread is toasted and cheddar liquefies, around 1 to 2 minutes for each side; rub barbecued bread with garlic clove.

Nutrition Information: Calories 351g, Fat 15.5g, Carbs 33.3g, Sugar 3.4g, Protein 20.7g

Grilled Ham and Cheese with Rosemary

Prep Time: 10mins, Cooking Time: 10mins
Serving: 2, Smart Point: 17

Ingredients:

- 2 tsp low fat cream cheese
- 2 tsp Dijon mustard
- 1 tsp Rosemary
- ¼ cups Swiss cheese
- ¼ cups part-skim mozzarella cheese
- 3 oz. extra lean
- 4 slices reduced-calorie whole wheat bread
- 2 sprays cooking spray

Instructions:

1. In a little bowl, consolidate cream cheddar, mustard, and rosemary. In another bowl, join the two sorts of cheddar.
2. Spot bread on a level surface and equally partition cream cheddar blend over each of the four bread cuts.
3. Top every one of two bread cuts with 2 tablespoons Gruyere blend and 1/2 ounces ham; sprinkle each with another 2 tablespoons Gruyere blend.
4. Spread sandwiches with outstanding bread cuts, spread-side down.
5. Coat a huge nonstick skillet with cooking shower and set over medium warmth.
6. Whenever hot, cook sandwiches until cheddar is softened, pushing down a couple of times, around 3 to 5 minutes for each side. Yields 1 sandwich for every serving.

Nutrition Information: Calories 420g, Fat 18g, Carbs 47g, Sugars 3g, Protein 11g

Turkey Taco Lettuce Wraps

Prep time: 10mins, Cooking Time: 10mins
Serving: 6, Smart Point: 6

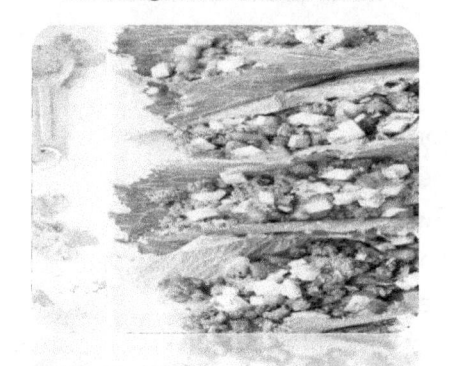

Ingredients:

- 1 - pound lean ground turkey
- 3 - tablespoons taco seasoning
- ½ - teaspoon kosher or sea salt
- 1 - cup cherry tomatoes, halved
- 1 - avocado, pitted, peeled, and diced
- 1 - cup salsa, no sugar added
- 12 - Whole romaine heat lettuce leaves

Instructions:

1. Add ground turkey to a skillet. Cook over medium warmth for 8 minutes until sautéed. Include 1/3 glass water, taco flavoring, and salt
2. Twofold every lettuce leaf so the best fits into the second and you have 6 multiplied leaves out and out.
3. Spoon in meat blend. Include cherry tomatoes and avocado pieces.
4. Top each with salsa.
5. Serve and appreciate

Nutrition Information: Calories 215g, Fat 13g, Carbs 11g, Sugars 4g, Protein 16g

Mushroom and Steak Fajita Sandwiches

Prep time: 15mins, Cooking Time: 25mins
Serving: 4, Smart Point: 11

Ingredients:

- 1 - tablespoon plus 2 teaspoons olive oil
- 1 - medium red onion, sliced in to strips
- 2 - cloves garlic
- 1 - medium red bell pepper
- 1 - pound beef sirloin tip steak
- 4 - ounces white mushrooms
- 2 - teaspoons dried oregano
- ½ - teaspoon black pepper
- Salt to taste
- 2 - whole wheat pita pockets cut in half
- 4 - leaves of Romaine lettuce
- ¼ - cup Greek yogurt, fat free, plain

Instructions:

1. Preheat broiler to 350 degrees.
2. In an expansive skillet, on medium-low warmth, sauté mushrooms in 1 tablespoon olive oil, around 6 minutes.
3. Include onions, garlic, and ringer peppers and keeps sautéing until onions and peppers are delicate around 4 minutes.
4. Include sirloin strips, and cook on medium warmth for around 5-10 minutes or until never again pink. Sprinkle with salt and pepper and oregano.
5. Blend well, spread and stew for 5 additional minutes. Channel blend.
6. Cut pita bread down the middle, brush remaining oil on all sides, place on a treated sheet for 3-5 minutes, sufficiently long to warm.

7. Stuff pita pockets with meat blend, romaine lettuce and best with a bit of yogurt or acrid cream.

Nutrition Information: Calories 424g, Fat 23g, Carbs 24g, Sugars 4g, Protein 30g

Heirloom Tomato Salad

Prep time: 25mins, Cooking Time: 15mins
Serving: 6, Smart Point: 6

Ingredients:

- 2 - tablespoons red wine vinegar
- 2 - tablespoons whole grain mustard
- ½ - teaspoon Kosher salt
- ¼ - cup olive oil
- 1 - teaspoon honey
- 4 - large heirloom tomatoes
- 1 - cup cubed low-fat fresh mozzarella
- ½ - cup fresh basil

Instructions:

1. In an extensive bowl, combine the vinegar, mustard, salt, oil, and nectar.
2. Consolidate well include the tomatoes, mozzarella, and basil.
3. Tenderly blend until all things are covered in the mustard blend. Serve and appreciate

Nutrition Information: Calories 162g, Fat 14g, Carbs 6g, Sugar 4g, Protein 5g

Wake Me Up, Keep Me Going Smoothie

Prep time: 10mins, Cooking Time: 15mins
Serving: 2, Smart Point: 8

Ingredients:

- 1 - frozen banana
- ½ - cup frozen grapes of any color
- ½ - avocado
- 1 - cup spinach
- 1 - cup kale, removes stem and discard
- 2 - tablespoons chia seeds
- 1 ½ - cups chilled green tea
- Ice if needed

Instructions:

1. Add all fixings to the blender, aside from ice, mix until smooth.
2. Include ice for a thicker smoothie.
3. Prescribe natural or homegrown spinach and kale.

Nutrition Information: Calories 226g, Fat 11g, Carbs 31g, Sugars 13g, Protein 5g

Asparagus Frittata with Herb Blossoms

Prep time: 20mins, Cooking Time: 35mins
Serving: 4, Smart Point: 5

Ingredients:

- 4 - asparagus spears
- 4 - eggs
- 2 - tablespoons grated Parmesan cheese
- ¼ - teaspoon salt
- 1/8 - teaspoon pepper
- 1 - chive blossoms
- 1 - sage blossom
- 2 - tablespoons extra virgin olive oil

Instructions:

1. In a pot of bubbling water, whiten the asparagus for 5 minutes.
2. Quickly submerge them in a bowl of ice water at that point let them cool. Channel the water when the asparagus has achieved room temperature.
3. Cleave then put aside.
4. In a bowl, set up the frittata by whisking the eggs with the Parmesan, salt, and pepper at that point put aside.
5. In a warm spot with the additional virgin olive oil, pour the frittata blend.
6. At the point when the frittata is mostly cooked, circulate the asparagus and the herb blooms.
7. At the point when the base part is cooked and the best part is as of now strong, turn the frittata by setting a plate over the pan, switch rapidly and let the frittata fall on the plate.
8. Set back the frittata on the pot cautiously by sliding it inside. Cook for one more moment.
9. Exchange the frittata to the serving plate and embellishment. Serve while hot.

Nutrition Information: Calories 147g, Fat 12g, Carbs 2g, Sugars 1g, Protein 7g

Crispy Mediterranean Vegetable Cakes

Prep time: 35mins, Cooking Time: 50mins
Serving: 4, Smart Point: 6

Ingredients:

- 2 - tablespoons olive oil
- 1 - small onion
- 2 - cloves garlic
- 3 - cups baby spinach
- 1 - medium potato, grated
- 1 - teaspoon dried oregano
- ¼ - cup chopped sun dried tomatoes
- ¼ - cup chopped Kalamata olives
- ¼ - cup chopped artichoke hearts
- ¼ - cup diced red bell pepper
- ¼ - cup diced yellow bell pepper
- 2 - eggs
- ¼ - cup whole wheat flour
- Sea salt and freshly ground pepper

Instructions:

1. Warmth a large portion of the olive oil in a substantial skillet over medium warmth.
2. Include the onion and cook until delicate. Include the garlic, and cook for one extra moment. Include the spinach and mix until shriveled. Turn off warmth and exchange to an expansive bowl.
3. Include the potato, oregano, tomatoes, olives, artichokes, and peppers to the medium blending bowl and mix. Include the eggs and flour, and season with salt and pepper.

4. Structure the blend into patties. Or on the other hand, if making as an entrée, structure into two extensive cakes.
5. Warmth the staying olive oil in a skillet and cooks the cakes until firm and seared on the two sides. Cut cakes into individual servings and serve hot.
6. Whenever wanted, top with an olive tapenade or slashed crisp herbs.

Nutrition Information: Calories 196g, Fat 11g, Carbs 20g, Sugars 2g, Protein 6g

Tomato, Hummus, and Spinach Sandwich

Prep time: 10mins, Cooking Time: 24mins
Serving: 2, Smart Point: 3

Ingredients:

- 2 - slices multigrain bread
- 2 - tablespoons roasted garlic hummus
- 3 - slices tomato
- ½ - cup baby spinach
- 1/8 - teaspoon salt

Instructions:

1. Toast multigrain bread.
2. Spread hummus over one cut of bread.
3. Top with tomato cuts and layer with spinach.

4. Sprinkle on salt. Spot the second cut of bread to finish everything. Serve and appreciate

Nutrition Information: Calories 100g, Fat 3g, Carbs 15g, Sugars 2g, Protein 5g

Baked Zucchini, Spinach, and Feta Casserole

Prep time: 15mins, Cooking Time: 30mins
Serving: 6, Smart Point: 5

Ingredients:

- 2 - tablespoons olive oil
- 3 - cups baby spinach
- 2 - small zucchini
- 2 - small yellow squash
- ¼ - cup fat free feta cheese
- ¼ - cup low-fat parmesan cheese
- ¼ cup panko bread crumbs
- 2 - egg whites
- ½ - teaspoon Kosher salt
- 2 - teaspoons garlic powder
- ½ - teaspoon ground black pepper
- 1 - teaspoon dried basil leaves

Instructions:

1. Preheat the broiler to four hundred stages. Bathe a 9 x 13-inchmeal dish with a non-stick splash and positioned apart.
2. In a sizeable skillet, warmness the olive oil. When warm, such as the spinach, zucchini, and yellow squash.
3. Cook, around 5mins, until the spinach, is withered and squash is sensitive.
4. Channel off any overabundance fluid and see in a good sized mixing bowl.

5. Add the rest of the fixings to blending bowl with the spinach combo.
6. Consolidate nicely and unfold the combination in a fair layer within the readied meal dish.
7. Heat for 30 to forty minutes or until notable darkish colored to finish the whole thing.
8. Let cool marginally earlier than serving.

Nutrition Information: Calories 162g, Fat 8g, Carbs 20g, Sugar 3g, Protein 6g

Meaty Veggie Roll-Ups

Prep Time: 23mins, Cooking Time: 35mins
Serving: 12, Smart Point: 1

Ingredients:

- 12 - thick slices unprocessed deli meat
- 1 - cup sliced vegetables
- 12 - chives

Instructions:

1. Spot wanted a measure of vegetables on a bit of shop meat.
2. Roll firmly, and whenever wanted, utilize a chive to tie. Pack in a zip-top plastic sack or sealed shut compartment.
3. Most loved Flavor Combinations:
4. Cook meat with red chile pepper strips, carrot sticks, and cucumber cuts with mustard for plunging.
5. Chicken with apple cuts, red cabbage, and pickle strips with Dijon mustard for plunging.
6. Turkey with disintegrated bacon and cut avocado with salsa for plunging.

Nutrition Information: Calories 71g, Fat 2.0g, Carbs 1.2g, Sugars 0.8g, Protein 11.3g

One Pot Turkey and Mediterranean Quinoa

Prep time: 15mins, Cooking Time: 55mins
Serving: 4, Smart Point: 4

Ingredients:

- 1 - tablespoon extra virgin olive oil
- 2 - cups nitrate free turkey rope sausage
- 2 - clove garlic, minced
- 1 - small yellow onion, cut into strips
- 1 - cup low sodium chicken broth
- 14 - ounce diced tomatoes
- ½ - teaspoon Kosher salt
- 1 ½ - cups quinoa, rinsed in cool water
- 2 - cups spinach
- ½ - cup low fat feta cheese

Instructions:

1. In expansive skillet, heat oil on medium warmth.
2. When hot, encompass turkey wiener, garlic, and onion.
3. Cook until onion starts to mollify.
4. Mix in soup, tomatoes, salt, and quinoa.
5. Heat to the factor of boiling and reduce to a stew and consist of spinach.

6. Keep on stewing, blending sporadically to maintain quinoa from staying, till juices is ingested.
7. Appreciate

Nutrition Information: Calories 117g, Fat 8g, Carbs 8g, Sugar 4g, Protein 5g

Skinny Burrito in a Jar

Prep time: 10mins, Cooking Time: 35mins
Serving: 4, Smart Point: 4

Ingredients:

- 1 - cup salsa, no sugar added
- 15 - ounce black beans
- 1 - cup reduced fat cheddar cheese
- ½ - cup Greek Yogurt, non-fat

Instructions:

1. Uniformly partition every fixing into 4 (1/2 diminutive) canning containers.
2. Include fixings in a specific order: 1/4 container salsa, 1/4 piling glass dark beans, 1/4 glass cheddar, and 2 tablespoons yogurt or acrid cream.
3. Refrigerate for as long as two days.
4. Eat straight from the container or add to an entire wheat wrap.

Nutrition Information: Calories 191g, Fat 2g, Carbs 27g, Sugars 6g, Protein 15g

Spring Mix with Roasted Pears and Feta

Prep time: 10mins, Cooking Time: 25mins
Serving: 4, Smart Point: 3

Ingredients:

- 8 - cups spring mix
- 1 - small red onion
- 2 - medium Bosc Pears
- 2 - teaspoons canola or olive oil
- ½ - cup feta cheese crumbles

Instructions:

1. Preheat broiler to 400 degrees.
2. Hurl pear wedges with oil and spot level side down, on a non-stick treat sheet.
3. Cook pears for 10 minutes, turn over and broil 10 extra minutes.
4. Permit to cool somewhat.
5. Join spring blend, onion and pears in an extensive plate of mixed greens bowl, sprinkle with feta and serve.

Nutrition Information: Calories 108g, Fat 0.3g, Carbs 24g, Sugars 11g, Protein 5g

Old-Fashioned Vegetable Soup

Prep time: 35mins, Cooking Time: 4hrs 35mins
Serving: 8, Smart Point: 4

Ingredients:

- 1 - cup fresh or frozen whole-kernel corn
- 1 - large potato
- 4 - carrots
- 1 - cup fresh or frozen green beans
- 1 - small sweet onion
- 1 - stalk celery
- ½ - teaspoon paprika
- ½ - teaspoon crushed red pepper flakes
- ½ - teaspoon black pepper
- Kosher or sea salt to taste
- 2 ½ - cups tomato juice
- 1 ½ - cups vegetable broth

Instructions:

1. Add all fixings to the moderate cooker, mix to join.
2. Spread and cook on low 8-10 hours.

Nutrition Information: Calories 116g, Fat 1g, Carbs 25g, Sugars 7g, Protein 4g

Hearty Kale Salad

Prep time: 20mins, Cooking Time: 35mins
Serving: 4, Smart Point: 6

Ingredients:

Salad:

- 2 - heads of kale, cut off the stem, washed and dried
- ½ - sweet potato, cubed and roasted
- ½ - cup pomegranate seeds

Dressing:

- 2 - Tbsp olive oil
- 2 - Tbsp lemon or lime juice
- Dash salt and pepper

Instructions:

1. Wash and get kale and cut dry stem, and set up the sweet potato and pomegranate seeds.
2. In a serving of mixed greens, bowl joins the kale, sweet potato, and pomegranate seeds.
3. In a different bowl combine the serving of mixed greens dressing and pour over the plate of mixed greens
4. Blend the serving of mixed greens dressing into the plate of mixed greens utilizing hands to knead the dressing into the kale-note that kale plate of mixed greens is substantially more tasteful after the kale has been adequately rubbed.
5. Serve the plate of mixed greens and appreciate

Nutrition Information: Calories 195g, Fat 15g, Carbs 12g, Sugar 3g, Protein 8g

No-Mayo Chicken Salad

Prep time: 20mins, Cooking Time: 15mins
Serving: 3, Smart Point: 6

Ingredients:

- 1 - pound chicken breast
- ¼ - cup extra-virgin olive oil
- 3 - tablespoons lemon juice
- ¼ - teaspoon kosher or sea salt
- ¼ - teaspoon black pepper
- 1 - cup cherry tomatoes
- ½ - cup diced celery
- 1 - tablespoon freshly chopped dill
- ¼ - cup freshly chopped parsley
- 6 - large savory (curly) cabbage leaves for serving

Instructions:

1. In a massive skillet over medium warm temperature, consist of 1 tablespoon olive oil, sauté chicken till terrific darkish colored.
2. While cooking the chicken, in a little bowl, combo last three tablespoon olive oil, lemon squeeze, salt, and pepper.
3. After bird turns amazing, change to a serving bowl and hurl in tomatoes, celery, dill, and parsley.
4. Shower with dressing and be part of, or serve as an afterthought.
5. Appreciate

Nutrition Information: Calories 438g, Fat 32g, Carbs 4g, Sugar 2g, Protein 32g

Mediterranean Tuna Salad

Prep time: 15mins, Cooking Time: 25mins
Serving: 2, Smart Point: 10

Ingredients:

- 6 - ounce or jar of tuna
- ½ - cup artichoke hearts
- ½ - cup pitted kalamata olives
- 1 - roasted red pepper
- ¼ - cup fresh chopped parsley
- 2 - tablespoons slivered basil leaves
- 3 - tablespoons olive oil
- Juice of 1 lemon
- Salt and fresh ground pepper

Instructions:

1. Join the majority of the fixings in a bowl and season with salt and pepper.
2. Chill until prepared to serve.
3. Serve in lettuce leaves, on a roll, or on entire grain wafers.

Nutrition Information: Calories 337g, Fat 25g, Carbs 14g, Sugars 3g, Protein 20g

Slow Cooker Turkey Sloppy Joes

Prep time: 45mins, Cooking Time: 3hrs 15mins
Serving: 4-6, Smart Point: 2

Ingredients:

- 454 – grams ground turkey breast
- 1 - cup onion, diced
- ½ - cup green pepper, diced
- 3 - cloves garlic, minced
- 1 - tablespoon yellow mustard
- ¼ - cup natural ketchup
- 8 – ounce no-salt added tomato sauce
- 1 - tablespoon BBQ sauce
- 1-2 - packets Stevia

Instructions:

1. Fog a skillet with oil and dark colored crude turkey, onions and inexperienced pepper over medium warmth.
2. Spot turkey meat, onions and green pepper inside the slight cooker.
3. Include the various fixings and blend properly.
4. Spread and prepare dinner on LOW for three-four hours or HIGH for two-three hours.
5. On the off chance which you don't darken the beef first, at that point cook dinner on LOW for five-6 hours or HIGH for 3-4 hours.
6. Present with a whole grain bun, toasted.

Nutrition Information: Calories 167g, Fat 4g, Carbs 14g, Sugars 8g, Protein 23g

Supermodel Superfood Salad

Prep time: 10mins, Cooking Time: 35mins
Serving: 6, Smart Point: 6

Ingredients:

One head of kale:

- ¼ - cup pine nuts
- ½ - cup dried cranberries
- Juice of 1 lemon
- ¼ - cup extra-virgin olive oil
- Pinch of kosher or sea salt

Instructions:

1. Evacuate and dispose of substantial stems of kale leaves.
2. Coarsely slash kale leaves and add to an expansive serving bowl.
3. Include pine nuts, dried cranberries or currants.
4. Crush the juice of one lemon, shower with olive oil, and sprinkle salt, hurl to join.
5. Whenever wanted, decorate with 1/4 container naturally ground parmesan cheddar.

Nutrition Information: Calories 162g, Fat 13g, Carbs 12g, Sugars 8g, Protein 2g

Cucumber, Dill, and Cream Cheese Sandwiches

Prep time: 28mins, Cooking Time: 30mins
Serving: 6, Smart Point: 5

Ingredients:

- 6 - ounces low fat cream cheese
- 1 - tablespoon fresh dill
- 2 - teaspoons finely grated lemon zest
- 6 - slices of whole wheat sandwich bread
- 1 - small or 1/2 big cucumber

Instructions:

1. In a little bowl, blend the cream cheddar, dill and lemon get-up-and-go.
2. Toast every one of the cuts of bread.
3. Spread the cream cheddar blend on each cut of bread at that point top with the cucumber.
4. Remove the sides of the bread. You can likewise quarter each cut to make chomp sizes.

Nutrition information: Calories 150g, Fat 5g, Carbs 20g, Sugars 3g, Protein 5g

Thai Chicken Lettuce Cups

Prep time: 22mins, Cooking Time: 40mins
Serving: 6-8, Smart Point: 1

Ingredients:

- 1 ½ - tablespoons cooking oil
- ½ - pound ground chicken breast
- 2 - shallots
- ¼ - red onion
- 1 - clove garlic
- Minced fresh chiles, Jalapeño
- 1 - tablespoon fish sauce
- ½ - lime, juiced
- 1 - teaspoon low-sodium soy sauce
- 1 - head iceberg lettuce
- 1 - handful of cilantro and/or mint

Instructions:

1. Warmth a wok or substantial sauté dish over high warmth. Whenever hot, whirl in 1 tablespoon of the oil and include the chicken.
2. Go through your spatula to break the meat and spread out over the outside of the container.
3. Cook until seared, around 3 minutes.
4. Drive the ground chicken to the other side of the skillet and whirl in the remaining ½ tablespoon of oil.
5. To the oil, include the shallots, red onion, garlic, and crisp chiles and sauté the aromatics until fragrant, around 30 seconds.
6. Include the fish sauce, lime juice, and soy sauce.
7. Present with lettuce mugs and herbs

Nutrition Information: Calories 120g, Fat 6.4g, Carbs 4.1g, Sugars 1.6g, Protein 11.9g

Tomatoes, Blueberries & Fennel Salad

Prep time: 25mins, Cooking Time: 15mins
Serving: 2, Smart Point: 6

Ingredients:

- 1 - cup cherry or grape tomatoes
- ½ - cup blueberries
- 1 - fennel bulb
- Extra virgin olive oil
- Squeeze of lemon
- Salt

Instructions:

1. In a bowl, hurl the tomatoes, fennel, and blueberries together.
2. Sprinkle with additional virgin olive oil and lemon squeeze at that point include the salt.
3. In a bowl, hurl the tomatoes, fennel, and blueberries together.

Nutrition Information: Calories 167g, Fat 11g, Carbs 19g, Sugars 6g, Protein 3g

Open Face Grilled Turkey Burgers

Prep time: 13mins, Cooking Time: 25mins
Serving: 6, Smart Point: 4

Ingredients:

- 1 - tablespoon olive oil, divided
- 2 - tablespoons green onions
- ½ - cup finely chopped mushrooms
- 1 - clove garlic, minced
- 1 - pound lean ground turkey
- ½ - teaspoon sea salt
- ½ - teaspoon black pepper
- 2 - cups baby spinach
- 1 - medium tomato, sliced into 6 rounds

Instructions:

1. Warmth olive oil in a skillet over medium-low warmth.
2. Include the green onions and mushrooms and cook until delicate and dark colored, around 5 minutes. Include the garlic and cook for 1 extra moment.
3. Turn off warmth and permit to cool marginally.

4. Include the turkey in an extensive bowl and include the mushroom blend, salt, and pepper.
5. Blend until well and structure into 6 patties.
6. Preheat a flame broil to medium-high warmth.
7. Shower gently with cooking splash and barbecue the burgers until cooked through, 6-8 minutes for each side.
8. Top the spinach with burgers includes tomato cuts and serves right away.

Nutrition Information: Calories 143g, Fat 9g, Carbs 2g, Sugars 1g, Protein 15g

Monte Cristo Sandwiches

Prep Time: 10mins, Cook Time: 8mins
Serving: 4, Smart Point: 10

Ingredients:

- 1 - huge egg
- 1 - egg white
- ½ - container non-fat milk
- 4 - tsp dijon mustard
- 8 - cut tough entire wheat bread
- 4 - oz low-fat skinless cooked turkey bosom

Instruction

1. Beat egg, egg white, and milk in a pie plate or wide, shallow bowl.
2. Spread mustard on 4 cups of bread. Layer with cheddar and turkey, top with residual cuts of bread, and press together firmly.
3. Splash an extensive nonstick skillet with cooking shower; heat over medium warmth.
4. Each one in turn, plunge each sandwich in the egg blend to coat, at that point place it in the hot container.

5. Cook, pushing down with a spatula, until daintily darker on the two sides, around 4 minutes for each side.

Nutritional Information: Calories 323g, Fat 13g, Carbs 25g, Sugars 5g, Protein 26g

Tuna Salad

Prep Time: 10mins, Cook Time: 5mins
Serving: 4, Smart Point: 3

Ingredients:

- 12 – oz. canned chunk solid white tuna in water
- ½ - cup celery
- 2 - tbsp fresh parsley
- 2 - tbsp reduced calorie mayonnaise
- ½ - tsp dijon mustard
- ½ - tsp salt
- ¼ - tsp black pepper

Instructions:

1. Join fish, celery, and parsley in a medium bowl.
2. Include mayonnaise, mustard, salt, and pepper; blend to consolidate.
3. For a flavor support without expanding the point's esteem.
4. Include diced olives, hacked pickles or relish, or onions.

Nutritional Information: Calories 137g, Fat 5g, Carbs 1g, Sugars 1g, Protein 20g

◈ WEIGHT WATCHERS DINNER RECIPES ◈

Roasted Cauliflower Soup

Prep time: 40mins, Cooking Time: 1hr 25mins
Serving: 4, Smart Point: 7

Ingredients:

- 14 - ounce cauliflower head
- ½ - teaspoon salt
- Pepper
- 1 - tablespoon extra virgin olive oil
- 1 - medium onion
- 1 - stalk celery
- 4 - cups vegetable broth
- ½ - teaspoon fresh rosemary
- ½ - cup water

Instructions:

1. Preheat stove to 395 degrees F.
2. On a preparing dish fixed with material paper, disperse the cauliflower.
3. Sprinkle with salt and pepper at that point shower with additional virgin olive oil. Prepare in the preheated broiler for 30 minutes.
4. Following 30 minutes, over medium warmth, sauté the onions and celery in a pot with additional virgin olive oil.

5. Include the broiled cauliflower at that point hurl for around 5 minutes.
6. Include the vegetable soup and rosemary and cook for an additional 15 minutes.
7. With the inundation blender, mix the soup until smooth and rich in the pot. Season with salt and pepper at that point cook for 5 additional minutes.
8. Serve in mugs at that point shower with additional virgin olive oil before serving.

Nutrition Information: Calories 231g, Fat 8g, Carbs 35g, Sugars 7g, Protein 8g

Chicken and Black Bean Chili

Prep time: 35mins, Cooking Time: 1hr 15mins
Serving: 6, Smart Point: 2

Ingredients:

- 1 - pound skinless boneless chicken breasts
- 15 - ounce black beans
- 1 - jalapeno or chili pepper of choice
- ½ - cup chopped bell pepper
- ½ - cup chopped carrots
- ½ - cup sliced celery
- 15 - ounce diced fire roasted tomatoes with juice
- 2 - cups chicken broth, low-sodium preferred
- 2 - garlic cloves
- ¼ - cup chopped onion
- 2 - teaspoons chili powder
- 2 - teaspoons cumin
- 1 - bay leaf
- 2- ½ - tablespoons olive oil
- ¼ - cup coarsely chopped cilantro
- ½ - teaspoon salt

Instructions:

1. Sauté hen in one tablespoon of olive oil over medium warm temperature for 8 to 10 minute.
2. Expel the chicken from the box and put aside.
3. Include 1-half tablespoons of olive oil and onions, Chile peppers, carrots, and celery over medium warm temperature till the onion is mellowed and translucent.
4. Include the minced garlic and cook dinner for 30 seconds to a second till remarkable and fragrant.
5. Include the juices, tomatoes in fluid, dark beans, flavors and, fowl, blend properly.
6. Stew over low warm temperature, quite secured, for 45mins to 60 minutes or till carrots are sensitive.
7. Present with any of the accompanying garnishes, each time wanted: meagerly reduce/diced hot bean stew peppers, plain low-fats Greek yogurt, low-fats cheddar, cut scallions, or disintegrated heated tortilla chips.

Nutrition Information: Calories 266g, Fat 9g, Carbs 21g, Sugars 4g, Protein 25g

Crock Pot Low-Fat Beef Stew

Prep time: 45mins, Cooking Time: 25mins
Serving: 6, Smart Point: 7

Ingredients:

- 1 - pound lean hamburger stew meat
- 2 - tablespoons flour for covering the meat
- 1 - container red wine
- 1 - teaspoon salt
- ½ - teaspoon dark pepper
- 2 - tablespoons additional virgin olive oil
- 1 - medium onion
- 1 - clove garlic
- 2 - medium potatoes

- ➢ 2 - medium carrots
- ➢ 2 - celery stalks
- ➢ ½ - container diced red peppers
- ➢ 2 - sound leaves
- ➢ 6 - sprigs of thyme
- ➢ 2 - mugs meat soup
- ➢ 14 - ounce fire-cooked diced tomatoes

Instructions:

1. Coat the meat with the flour at that factor shake off the overabundance at that point sprinkle half teaspoon salt and 1/four teaspoon dark pepper.
2. Over medium warmth, in a pan with extra virgin olive oil, dark colored the floured hamburger at that factor pour within the wine.
3. Cook until sauce is fairly thickened and liquor odor is long gone around 5 minutes.
4. Exchange the hamburger and its sauce to the stewing pot.
5. In the gradual cooker, such as onion, garlic, potatoes, carrots, celery, purple peppers, leaves from four thyme sprigs, cove leaves, stock, tomatoes, and the rest of the half of teaspoon salt and pepper. Spread and cook dinner on low for eight hours or excessive 4 - 6 hours.
6. Enhancement with staying two thyme sprigs.

Nutrition Information: Calories 264g, Fat 8g, Carbs 24g, Sugars 4g, Protein 18g

Farro & Cranberry Bean Soup

Prep time: 35mins, Cooking Time: 35mins
Serving: 4, Smart Point: 6

Ingredients:

- 1- ½ - cups cranberry/borlotti beans
- 1 - cup farro, soaked for 2 hours & drained
- 1 - cup tomato puree
- 2 - cloves garlic
- 1 - celery stalk
- 1 - carrot
- 1 - small or 1/2 big onion
- 2 - twigs fresh rosemary
- ¼ - teaspoon salt
- ¼ - teaspoon pepper
- 2- ½ - tablespoons extra virgin olive oil

Instructions:

1. Heat up the farro in salted water for 30 minutes at that point channel, dispose of the water and put the farro aside.
2. In another pan, over medium warmth, heat up the beans with rich water, 1 twig of rosemary, 1 clove garlic, 1

tablespoon additional virgin olive oil, salt, and pepper. Cook until the beans are delicate, around 60 minutes.
3. Dispose of the rosemary and garlic.
4. Exchange half of the beans to a blender at that point mix until smooth. Put aside.
5. In a third pan with 1 tablespoon additional virgin olive oil, over medium warmth, sauté the rest of the garlic, celery, carrots, and onions.
6. After around 10mins, including the tomato puree at that point put down the fire.
7. Still in the pan with the tomato puree, over low warmth, includes the smooth and entire beans.
8. Spoon a portion of the stock of the beans to keep a smooth and soupy consistency. Continue adding the stock to keep a similar consistency.
9. Include the farro then season with salt and pepper. Cook for an additional 5 minutes. Dispose of the rosemary.
10. Prior to serving, sprinkle with staying additional virgin olive oil. Serve hot.

Nutrition Information: Calories 181g, Fat 10g, Carbs 19g, Sugars 3g, Protein 5g

Slow Cooker Savory Superfood Soup

Prep time: 55mins, Cooking Time: 45mins
Serving: 8, Smart Point: 1

Ingredients:

- 2 - cups sliced carrots
- 1 - large sweet potato
- 1 - cup fresh or frozen green beans
- ½ - cup fresh cilantro
- 1 - small onion
- 1 - clove garlic
- 15 - ounce black beans, drained and rinsed

- ½ - teaspoon crushed red pepper flakes
- ½ - teaspoon black pepper
- 1 - teaspoon chili powder
- 1 - teaspoon cumin
- Kosher or sea salt to taste
- 2 - cups vegetable juice
- 2 - cups vegetable broth

Instructions:

1. Join all fixings within the slight cooker, unfold and prepare dinner on low 6-eight hours, or until greens are sensitive.
2. Include a tablespoon of diminished fats cheddar, on every occasion wanted.
3. On the off threat which you incline toward a greater obvious onion and garlic paste, sauté onion in 1 tablespoon olive oil till delicate, around 5 minutes.
4. Include garlic and sauté 1 extra moment. Add to mild cooker along distinctive fixings.
5. To make this plenty to an extra quantity a Super-food Soup.
6. Includes 2 glasses coarsely slashed kale the maximum recent 5mins of cooking, or till withered.

Nutrition Information: Calories 157g, Fat 1g, Carbs 32g, Sugars 6g, Protein 7g

Slow Cooker Chicken Chili

Prep time: 30mins, Cooking Time: 25mins
Serving: 10, Smart Point: 1

Ingredients:

- 2 - cloves garlic
- ½ - cup diced sweet onion
- 2 -3 - chicken breast fillets
- 14.5 - ounce fire roasted tomatoes with liquid

- 6 - ounce tomato paste
- 1 ½ - cups chicken broth
- 2 - tablespoons chili powder
- ½ - teaspoon cayenne pepper
- ½ - teaspoon cumin
- ½ - teaspoon black pepper
- Kosher or sea salt to taste
- 15.5 - ounce Cannellini
- 15.5 - ounce Kidney beans
- ¼ - cup reduced fat cheddar cheese for garnish

Instructions:

1. Join all the above fixings in the moderate cooker.
2. Spread and cook on low 8 hours in a 4-6 quart moderate cooker.
3. Spoon into dishes and top with a little cheddar and diced onion, whenever wanted.
4. The chicken utilized in this formula was crude while going in the moderate cooker.
5. On the off chance that you as of now have cooked chicken, simply include it around an hour prior as far as possible of cooking time.

Nutrition Information: Calories 222g, Fat 4g, Carbs 23g, Sugars 5g, Protein 24g

Slow Cooker Turkey Stew

Prep time: 40mins, Cooking Time: 30mins
Serving: 6, Smart Point: 4

Ingredients:

- 1 - stalk celery
- ½ - cup diced onion
- 2 - cloves garlic
- 1 - large potato
- 2 - carrots
- ½ - teaspoon black pepper
- ½ - teaspoon crushed red pepper flakes
- 1 - cup frozen peas
- 2 - cups chicken broth
- 14.5 - oz. fire roasted tomatoes
- Kosher or sea salt to taste
- 2 - cups (cooked) leftover turkey

Instructions:

1. Include all the above fixings, aside from turkey to the moderate cooker, blend to join.
2. Spread and cook on low 8 hours or until carrots are delicate.
3. Include extra turkey, the most recent 30 minutes of cooking time and cook until warmed through.

Nutrition Information: Calories 183g, Fat 4g, Carbs 17g, Sugars 5g, Protein 21g

Slow Cooker Chicken Gyros

Prep time: 1hr 10mins, Cooking Time: 2hrs 35mins
Serving: 8, Smart Point: 7

Ingredients:

- ½ - small onion
- 3 - cloves garlic
- 2 - pounds ground chicken
- 2 - eggs, whisked
- ½ - cup plain whole wheat breadcrumbs
- 1 - lemon, juiced and zested
- 1 - teaspoon dried thyme
- ¼ - teaspoon cinnamon
- ¼ - teaspoon nutmeg
- 2 - teaspoons salt
- 1 - tablespoon extra virgin olive oil
- 6 – inch whole wheat naan or pita bread rounds

Instructions:

1. In a sustenance processor, beat onion and garlic until pureed.
2. In an expansive bowl, mix together onion puree, ground chicken, eggs, breadcrumbs, lemon, thyme, cinnamon, nutmeg, and salt.
3. Combine until very much consolidated.
4. Structure into an expansive ball and spot in a 4-quart stewing pot which has been showered with olive oil.
5. Spread and cook for 4-6 hours on high, or 6-8 hours on low.
6. Unplug simmering pot and evacuate cover 30 minutes before serving.
7. This will enable the gyros to set and cut into decent cuts.
8. At the point when prepared to serve, expel meat from moderate cooker.

9. Cut and serve on warmed pita bread finished with tomatoes, cucumbers, yogurt, and crisp crushed lemon juice. Appreciate

Nutrition Information: Calories 248g, Fat 13g, Carbs 10g, Sugars 2g, Protein 23g

Zucchini Noodles Aglio et Olio

Prep time: 20mins, Cooking Time: 45mins
Serving: 2, Smart Point: 7

Ingredients:

- 4 - zucchini
- ½ - teaspoon coconut oil
- 2 - tablespoons extra-virgin olive oil
- 2 - cloves garlic
- ¼ - teaspoon crushed red pepper flakes
- ¼ - cup fresh parsley leaves
- salt and black pepper

Instructions:

1. Spot the julienned zucchini in a colander or wire strainer and hurl liberally with salt until the strands are softly covered. Enable the zucchini to sit for 20-30 minutes to evacuate abundance water. Wash with running water, channel well, and pat dry with paper towels.
2. While the zucchini is perspiring in the colander, heat a huge skillet over medium-high warmth, around 2 minutes. Include the coconut oil, and when it's dissolved include the almond flour and a spot of salt. Sauté, mixing regularly with a wooden spoon, until it's toasty dark colored, around 2 minutes. Expel scraps from the dish and put something aside for enhancement.
3. Return the container to medium-high warmth and include the readied zucchini noodles. Sauté them in the dry skillet,

until simply delicate, around 1-2 minutes. Push the noodles to the side of the skillet, and lessen the warmth to low. Include the olive oil, garlic, and pulverized red pepper, blending with the spoon until the garlic is fragrant, around 20 seconds. Drive the zucchini noodles into the oil, and mix delicately until they're covered. Turn off the warmth and blend the parsley, salt, and dark pepper into the noodles.

4. Sprinkle the noodles with the almond flour pieces before serving. Slurping and incredibly enormous chomps are healthily empowered.

Nutrition Information: Calories 190g, Fat 16g, Carbs 10g, Sugars 6g, Protein 3g

Grilled Turkey Veggie Burger
Prep time: 15mins, Cooking Time: 30mins
Serving: 6, Smart Point: 6

Ingredients:

- 1 - pound lean ground turkey
- 1 - cup grated carrot

- 1 - cup grated zucchini
- 2 - cloves garlic, minced
- ½ - teaspoon black pepper
- Kosher or sea salt to taste
- 2 - teaspoons olive oil
- 6 - slices whole grain artisan bread
- 6 - Romaine heart lettuce leafs
- 1 - medium tomato

Instructions:

1. In an extensive blending, bowl consolidates the initial six fixings and shape into 6 patties.
2. Patties can be cooked on an open-air flame broil, frying pan, skillet or stove oven.
3. Cook patties over medium warmth for about around 12 minutes or until there is never again any pink shading.
4. While the burger is cooking, brush olive oil more than one side of bread.
5. Cuts and either sear in the broiler, place on a frying pan or skillet and cook until brilliant and firm.
6. Add most loved fixings to the burger and serve right away.
7. Attempt our Goat Cheese Yogurt Spread, highlighted in the Turkey Veggie Burger photograph.

Nutrition Information: Calories 228g, Fat 10g, Carbs 15g, Sugars 4g, Protein 19g

Mushroom and Steak Fajita Sandwiches

Prep time: 25mins, Cooking Time: 35mins
Serving: 4, Smart Point: 11

Ingredients:

- 1 - tablespoon plus 2 teaspoons olive oil
- 1 - medium red onion
- 2 - cloves garlic
- 1 - medium red bell pepper
- 1 - pound beef sirloin tip steak
- 4 - ounces white mushrooms
- 2 - teaspoons dried oregano
- ½ - teaspoon black pepper
- Salt to taste
- 2 - whole wheat pita pockets cut in half
- 4 - leaves of Romaine lettuce
- ¼ - cup Greek yogurt

Instructions:

1. Preheat broiler to 350 degrees.
2. In an expansive skillet, on medium-low warmth, sauté mushrooms in 1 tablespoon olive oil, around 6 minutes.
3. Include onions, garlic, and ringer peppers and keeps sautéing until onions and peppers are delicate around 4 minutes.
4. Include sirloin strips, and cook on medium warmth for around 5-10 minutes or until never again pink.
5. Sprinkle with salt and pepper and oregano. Mix well, spread and stew for 5 additional minutes. Channel blend.
6. Cut pita bread down the middle, brush remaining oil on all sides, place on a treated sheet for 3-5 minutes, sufficiently long to warm.
7. Stuff pita pockets with meat blend, romaine lettuce and best with a bit of yogurt or acrid cream.

Nutrition Information: Calories 424g, Fat 23g, Carbs 24g, Sugars 4g, Protein 30g

Turkey Taco Lettuce Wraps

Prep time: 20mins, Cooking Time: 20mins
Serving: 6, Smart Point: 6

Ingredients:

- 1 - pound lean ground turkey
- 3 - tablespoons taco seasoning
- ½ - teaspoon kosher or sea salt
- 1 - cup (half-pint) cherry tomatoes
- 1 - avocado, pitted
- 1 - cup salsa, no sugar added
- 12 - Whole romaine heat lettuce leaves

Instructions:

1. Add ground turkey to a skillet. Cook over medium warmth for 8 minutes until sautéed.
2. Include 1/3 container water, taco flavoring, and salt
3. Permit to cook for 3 minutes more.
4. Twofold every lettuce leaf so the best fits into the second and you have 6 multiplied leaves by and large.
5. Spoon in meat blend. Include cherry tomatoes and avocado pieces. Top each with salsa.
6. Serve and appreciate

Nutrition Information: Calories 215g, Fat 13g, Carbs 11g, Sugars 4g, Protein 16g

Tomato, Hummus, and Spinach Sandwich

Prep time: 40mins, Cooking Time: 35mins
Serving: 2, Smart Point: 3

Ingredients:

- 2 - slices multigrain bread
- 2 - tablespoons roasted garlic hummus
- 3 - slices tomato
- ½ - cup baby spinach
- 1/8 - teaspoon salt

Instructions:

1. Toast multigrain bread.
2. Spread hummus over one cut of bread. Top with tomato cuts and layer with spinach.
3. Sprinkle on salt.
4. Spot the second cut of bread to finish everything. Serve and appreciate

Nutrition Information: Calories 100g, Fat 3g, Carbs 15g, Sugars 2g, Protein 5g

Skinny Tacos with Guacamole and Grilled Chicken

Prep time: 35mins, Cooking Time: 45mins
Serving: 4, Smart Point: 5

Ingredients:

- 1 - avocado
- 1/8 - cup fresh lime juice
- ¼ - teaspoon salt
- 1 - medium red onion
- 2 - big red tomatoes
- 8 - ounces filleted white chicken meat
- Salad leaves
- 4 - hard taco shells

Instructions:

1. Change the salt if fundamental.
2. Incorporate the minced red onion and minced tomatoes.
3. Mix well at that segment situated aside.
4. Over medium-intemperate warmth, on a skillet or barbecue fire sear, grills the two aspects of the fledgling till cooked by means of.
5. Finish off the taco shells with the plate of joined vegetable leaves, guacamole, feathered creature, decrease tomatoes and onions.

Nutrition Information: Calories 174g, Fat 9g, Carbs 11g, Sugars 4g, Protein 14g

Slow Cooker Spinach Artichoke Chicken

Prep time: 1hr 45mins, Cooking Time: 45mins
Serving: 4, Smart Point: 5

Ingredients:

- 8 - cups loosely packed spinach
- 1 - cup chicken broth
- 6-8 - ounce whole chicken breasts
- 3 - cloves fresh garlic
- ¼ - sweet onion
- 4 - tablespoons cream cheese
- 4 - tablespoons parmesan cheese
- 14 - ounce artichoke hearts
- 1 - cup chopped grape
- salt and pepper to taste

Instructions:

1. Spot spinach, chicken soup, and chicken bosoms in 4-quart moderate cooker.
2. Sprinkle with garlic, onion, and salt and pepper.
3. Spread and cook on low for 6-8 hours, or on high from 4-6 hours.
4. Just before serving, tenderly expel chicken bosoms from the moderate cooker and spot on serving platters.
5. Blend in cream cheddar, parmesan cheddar, and artichokes. Mix until velvety. Spoon sauce over chicken.
6. Top with tomatoes. Sprinkle with additional parmesan cheddar, whenever wanted.

Nutrition Information: Calories 246g, Fat 6g, Carbs 14g, Sugars 3g, Protein 35g

Salmon with Ginger Noodles

Prep time: 25mins, Cooking Time: 35mins
Serving: 4, Smart Point: 7

Ingredients:

- 8 – ounce salmon steaks
- 2 - tablespoons olive oil
- 1/8 - teaspoon salt
- Freshly ground black pepper
- 4 - ounces rice noodles
- 1 - tablespoon grated ginger root
- 1 - tablespoon sesame oil
- 1 - mustard oil
- 1 - radish
- 1 - tablespoon sesame seeds
- 1 - tablespoon chopped mint
- 2 - tablespoons coconut milk

Instructions:

1. Preheat flame broil to medium-high. Or then again 375 tiers F.
2. On the off chance that searing, preheat the grill.

3. Oil the meshes of the flame broil. On the off risk that searing, line a getting ready sheet with aluminum foil, and bathe with a nonstick cooking splash.
4. Brush salmon steaks with oil. Sprinkle with salt and pepper.
5. In the event that searing, vicinity filet pores and skin face down on the sheet and prepare dinner for 3 to five minutes, at that point flip and cook dinner for a further 3 to 5 minutes, or till fish is hazy inside the middle and drops efficiently with a fork.
6. In the occasion that flames broiling, area the salmon pores and skin-side down at the oiled meshes, unfold and cook dinner for 10 to fifteen minutes till fish is murky within the inside and drops efficiently with a fork.
7. Partition each salmon steak into same components to make four servings.
8. In a touch pot over low warm temperature, consolidate the cooked noodles, sesame oil, and mustard oil, if making use of. Mix in coconut milk and season.
9. Sprinkle cut radishes, mint leaves, and toasted sesame seeds over noodles.
10. Gap each salmon steak down the middle to make four servings.
11. Spot warm noodles on plates and high-quality with salmon steaks.

Nutrition Information: Calories 246g, Fat 21g, Carbs 1g, Sugars 0.2g, Protein 13g

Oven-Grilled Salmon

Prep time: 15mins, Cooking Time: 25mins
Serving: 4, Smart Point: 7

Ingredients:

- 3-4 - ounce each salmon fillets
- 2 - tablespoons olive oil
- ½ - teaspoon salt
- ½ - teaspoon pepper

Instructions:

1. Preheat broiler to 450 degrees.
2. Spot salmon on material lined or nonstick heating sheet.
3. Shower with oil and sprinkle with salt and pepper.
4. Heat for 12 to 15 minutes, until salmon is cooked through.

Nutrition Information: Calories 267g, Fat 20g, Carbs 0.2g, Sugars 0.4g, Protein 20g

Slow Cooker Herb Chicken and Vegetables

Prep time: 20mins, Cooking Time: 40mins
Serving: 6, Smart Point: 3

Ingredients:

- 1 - carrot
- 1 - parsnip
- 1 - pound small red potatoes
- 3 - garlic cloves
- 1 - yellow onion
- 3 - bone-in, split chicken breast
- ¼ - cup extra-virgin olive oil
- 1 - teaspoon paprika
- ½ - teaspoon black pepper
- Kosher or sea salt to taste
- 2 - tablespoon fresh parsley

- 1 - tablespoon fresh sage
- 1 - tablespoon fresh thyme
- 1 - tablespoon fresh rosemary

Instructions:

1. Include carrots, parsnips, potatoes onion and garlic to a medium mixing bowl.
2. In a touch bowl, consolidate oil, paprika, herbs, salt, and pepper.
3. Include half of oil and herb mixture to greens, hurl to coat and add to mild cooker.
4. Wash and pat hen dry, add to the mixing bowl and pour ultimate oil and herb mixture over chicken, being certain to completely coat.
5. In a big skillet, swing to medium-excessive warmth, encompass chook and lightly darker the 2 aspects.
6. Spot bird over veggies, spread and cook dinner on low five-6 hours or till juices run clear while pierced with a fork, or chook has completed an inward temperature of a hundred sixty five tiers and veggies are delicate.

Nutrition Information: Calories 207g, Fat 10g, Carbs 23g, Sugars 3g, Protein 7g

Spicy Asian Chicken Meatballs

Prep time: 25mins, Cooking Time: 45mins
Serving: 18, Smart Point: 7

Ingredients:

- 1 - pound (lean) ground chicken
- 1 - egg
- ½ - cup whole-wheat bread crumbs
- 1 - tablespoon Red Pepper powder or flakes
- ½ - cup green onions, finely diced
- 2 - teaspoons garlic powder
- 2 - teaspoons fresh
- ¾ - teaspoon kosher salt
- 3 - tablespoons honey
- 3 - tablespoons apple cider vinegar
- 3 - tablespoons tamari
- 1 - tablespoon sesame seeds
- 2 - tablespoons fresh cilantro

Instructions:

1. Preheat stove to 350 degrees.
2. In a substantial bowl, combine ground chicken, egg, bread pieces, red pepper drops, green onions, garlic powder, ginger, and salt.
3. Put aside for 15 minutes to enable the breadcrumbs to grow, at that point fold into 1" balls.

4. Spot on a material lined heating sheet and prepare for 18-22 minutes, or just until the focal point of every meatball is cooked.
5. Exchange meatballs to an expansive skillet.
6. In a little bowl, whisk together nectar, vinegar, and tamari.
7. Spread skillet and swing stove to medium warmth, blending each 2-3 minutes as expected to shield the meatballs from adhering to the base of the container.
8. Cook just until the blend starts to steam.
9. Expel from warmth, sprinkle with sesame seeds and cilantro.
10. Serve meatballs promptly and appreciate

Nutrition Information: Calories 221g, Fat 9g, Carbs 20g, Sugars 10g, Protein 17g

Mediterranean Tuna Salad

Prep time: 40mins, Cooking Time: 35mins
Serving: 2, Smart Point: 10

Ingredients:

- 6 - ounce or jar of tuna
- ½ - cup artichoke hearts
- ½ - cup pitted kalamata olives
- 1 - roasted red pepper
- ¼ - cup fresh chopped parsley
- 2 - tablespoons slivered basil leaves
- 3 - tablespoons olive oil
- Juice of 1 lemon
- Salt and fresh ground pepper

Instructions:

1. Merge most of the fixings in a bowl and season with salt and pepper.
2. Chill until sorted out to serve.

3. Serve in lettuce leaves, on a portion, or on total grain saltines.

Nutrition Information: Calories 337g, Fat 25g, Carbs 14g, Sugars 3g, Protein 20g

Southwestern Quinoa Salad

Prep time: 30mins, Cooking Time: 1hr 25mins
Serving: 8, Smart Point: 7

Ingredients:

- Quinoa Salad
- 1 - cup uncooked quinoa
- 1 - ripe avocado
- 1 - cup thawed corn kernels
- 15 - ounce black beans, drained and rinsed
- 1-½ - cups cherry tomatoes
- ¼ - cup coarsely chopped cilantro

Dressing:

- 2 - tablespoons extra-virgin olive oil
- 1 - tablespoon fresh squeezed lime juice
- 1 - teaspoon paprika
- 1/8 - teaspoon cayenne pepper
- ½ - teaspoon kosher or sea salt

Instructions:

1. Bring 1/2 containers water and quinoa to a bubble. Decrease warmth to the most minimal setting and spread.
2. Permit to cook for 15 minutes or until all water is consumed. Turn off warmth and leave quinone spread on the burner for 5-10 minutes.
3. Cushion with a fork.
4. Chill quinoa in the cooler for no less than 1 hour or medium-term.

5. Prepare cooled quinoa with the rest of the plate of mixed greens fixings. Whisk together dressing fixings.
6. Add dressing to a plate of mixed greens and hurl to consolidate. Serve and appreciate

Nutrition Information: Calories 226g, Fat 9g, Carbs 31g, Sugar 2g, Protein 8g

Fresh & Hearty Salad

Prep time: 20mins, Cooking Time: 25mins
Serving: 4, Smart Point: 5

Ingredients:

- 6 - containers child blended plate of mixed greens
- 1 - green chile pepper
- 1 - container jolted
- 1 - container split cherry tomatoes
- ¼ - container cut almonds
- ½ - container defrosted
- 1 - tablespoon additional virgin olive oil
- ½ - teaspoon dried oregano
- ½ - teaspoon Dijon mustard
- ¼ - teaspoon legitimate
- ¼ - teaspoon dark pepper

Instructions:

1. Whisk together oregano, red wine vinegar, Dijon mustard, salt, and pepper.
2. Gradually shower in olive oil, whisking while at the same time pouring.
3. Prepare all serving of mixed greens fixings together in a huge plate of mixed greens bowl.
4. Include plate of mixed greens dressing and hurl or serve as an afterthought.
5. Appreciate

Nutrition Information: Calories 129g, Fat 7g, Carbs 14g, Sugar 8g, Protein 5g

Supermodel Superfood Salad

Prep time: 15mins, Cooking Time: 35mins
Serving: 6, Smart Point: 6

Ingredients:

- One head of kale
- ¼ - cup pine nuts
- ½ - cup dried cranberries or currants
- Juice of 1 lemon
- ¼ - cup extra-virgin olive oil
- Pinch of kosher

Instructions:

1. Evacuate and dispose of substantial stems of kale leaves.
2. Coarsely hack kale leaves and add to an extensive serving bowl.
3. Include pine nuts, dried cranberries or currants.
4. Crush the juice of one lemon, shower with olive oil, and sprinkle salt, hurl to consolidate.

5. Whenever wanted, decorate with 1/4 container newly ground parmesan cheddar.

Nutrition Information: Calories 162g, Fat 13g, Carbs 12g, Sugars 8g, Protein 2g

Kale and Roasted Yam Salad

Prep time: 30mins, Cooking Time: 35mins
Serving: 4, Smart Point: 7

Ingredients:

- 1 - bunch lacinato
- 1 - sweet potato
- 1 - tablespoon extra virgin olive oil
- 1 - ripe avocado, peeled, pitted and cut into slices
- 2 - teaspoons freshly squeezed lemon
- 1 - tablespoon sesame seeds
- 1/3 - cup pumpkin or shelled sunflower seeds
- 1 - cup (half pint) cherry or grape tomatoes
- ½ - teaspoon kosher or sea salt
- ¼ - teaspoon black pepper

Instructions:

1. Preheat broiler to 375 degrees. Hurl sweet potatoes in olive oil, 1/4 teaspoon of the salt, and 1/8 teaspoon pepper.
2. Spread on a material lined or nonstick heating sheet.
3. Cook for 25 minutes, flipping the pieces part of the way through, or until fork delicate and caramelized a bit.
4. Include kale, tomatoes, sweet potatoes, remaining 1/4 teaspoon salt, and 1/8 teaspoon dark pepper to a serving of mixed greens bowl and hurl.
5. Sweet potato pieces might be included warm or cool. Sprinkle the plate of mixed greens with sesame seeds and pumpkin seeds or sunflower seeds.

6. Tenderly prepare avocado cuts in lemon/lime squeeze, and extra best of the plate of mixed greens.
7. Appreciate with your most loved dressing or straightforward vinaigrette.

Nutrition Information: Calories 200g, Fat 13g, Carbs 21g, Sugars 5g, Protein 6g

Roast Butternut Squash and Chickpea Salad

Prep time: 35mins, Cooking Time: 45mins
Serving: 4, Smart Point: 7

Ingredients:

Salad:

- 1 - small 1 to 1-1/2 pound butternut squash
- 1- ¾ - cups cooked garbanzo beans
- 2 - cups spinach leaves
- Seeds from the butternut squash
- 1 - tablespoon olive oil or coconut oil
- ¼ - teaspoon salt
- ¼ - teaspoon pepper

Dressing

- 2 - tablespoons lime juice
- 2 - tablespoons soy sauce

- ➢ 1 - tablespoon virgin coconut oil

Instructions:

1. Preheat the broiler to 425 degrees. Line a sheet dish with material paper. Hurl squash with olive oil, salt, and pepper.
2. One corner of the sheet dish, include seeds with olive oil, salt, and pepper.
3. Seeds will be cooked following 5 to 10 minutes and can be expelled from the dish.
4. Cook squash for 20 to 25 minutes, until squash pieces are fork delicate.
5. Then, whisk together the dressing fixings.
6. Delicately hurl squash with garbanzo beans, greens, and dressing. Spot on a platter or in a serving of mixed greens bowl.
7. Top with toasted squash seeds and serve.

Nutrition Information: Calories 201g, Fat 8g, Carbs 30g, Sugars 5g, Protein 6g

6-Ingredient Mexican-Style Quinoa Salad

Prep time: 15mins, Cooking Time: 25mins
Serving: 4, Smart Point: 5

Ingredients:

- ➢ ½ - cup dry quinoa, pre-rinsed
- ➢ 15 - ounce black beans
- ➢ 1 - cups salsa, no-sugar added
- ➢ 1 - cup corn kernels
- ➢ 1 - teaspoon chili powder
- ➢ 1 - avocado

Instructions:

1. Include 1 container water and quinoa to a medium pot and convey to a moving bubble over medium-high warmth.
2. Diminish warmth to a stew, spread and cook until most dampness is assimilated around 12-15 minutes.
3. Turn off warmth and leave secured quinoa on the burner for 5 minutes.
4. Add to cooked quinoa, dark beans, salsa, corn, and stew powder. Add salt and pepper to taste.
5. Hurl to consolidate at that point include diced avocado and delicately hurl.
6. Add a plate of mixed greens to a serving dish and serve.
7. A plate of mixed greens can likewise be delighted in the virus.
8. Appreciate

Nutrition Information: Calories 323g, Fat 10g, Carbs 49g, Sugar 4g, Protein 13g

Avocado & Grape Salad with Walnuts

Prep time: 30mins, Cooking Time: 45mins
Serving: 4, Smart Point: 7

Ingredients:

- 1 - avocado
- 2 - tablespoons freshly-squeezed lemon juice
- 1 ½ - cups halved grapes
- 1/3 - cup coarsely chopped walnuts
- ½ - cup sliced celery
- 1 - package baby arugula or baby kale
- 1 - green apple, cored, quartered
- ¼ - teaspoon kosher or sea salt
- ¼ - teaspoon black pepper

Instructions:

1. Hurl avocado cuts in a single tablespoon lemon juice. Hurl apple cuts independently in outstanding tablespoon lemon juice.
2. Hurl grapes, walnuts, celery, apple, child kale or arugula, and salt and pepper together.
3. Cautiously include avocado and hurl.
4. Appreciate with a most loved clean eating plate of mixed greens dressing or vinaigrette served prepared in a plate of mixed greens or as an afterthought.

Nutrition Information: Calories 171g, Fat 9g, Carbs 23g, Sugar 15g, Protein 3g

Creamy Fennel Salad, Orange Wedge, Fresh Mint

Prep time: 1hr 25mins, Cooking Time: 55mins
Serving: 4, Smart Point: 6

Ingredients:

- 3 - medium-sized fennel bulbs
- 1 - lemon
- ¼ - cup olive oil

- ➢ 1 - tablespoon Dijon mustard
- ➢ 1 - teaspoon salt
- ➢ ½ - cup fresh mint leaves
- ➢ ¼ - cup chopped fennel fronds
- ➢ 1 - orange
- ➢ Freshly ground black pepper

Instructions:

1. Clean the fennel with the resource of washing the outside of the knob.
2. Shave the fennel with a mandolin or with a blade by using reducing carefully over the surface.
3. The fennel ought to be cut slim.
4. Hurl in a bowl with the mint, the ¼ diploma of the slashed fennel fronds and orange wedges.
5. Dressing Instructions:
6. In a bit bowl positioned the Dijon mustard and overwhelm in the juice of one lemon.
7. Gradually shower in the olive oil, rushing as you move.
8. Add salt to flavor, and maintain on racing till absolutely consolidated and velvety.
9. Sprinkle dressing over the plate of combined veggies and hurl to consolidate.
10. Sprinkle with newly ground dark pepper to flavor.

Nutrition Information: Calories 171g, Fat 13.2g, Carbs 14.8g, Sugars 1g, Protein 2.7g

Lasagna with Fresh Tomatoes and Zucchini

Prep time: 1hr 10mins, Cooking Time: 45mins
Serving: 6, Smart Point: 7

Ingredients:

- 10 - whole wheat or fortified
- 4 - ounces fresh or good quality part-skim or lower-fat mozzarella,
- 1 - cup skim or low-fat ricotta cheese
- ½ - cup finely grated Parmesan cheese
- 3 - cups coarsely chopped tomatoes
- ½ - teaspoon salt
- 2 - cloves garlic, minced
- 2 - tablespoons extra virgin olive oil
- 1 - medium yellow or green zucchini
- ½ - tablespoon Italian seasoning

Instructions:

1. Preheat the broiler to 375 degrees F.
2. In a little bowl, combine ricotta, squash, 1/4 measure of the Parmesan, and half of the mozzarella.
3. Puree the tomatoes, salt, garlic, Italian flavoring or crisp herbs, and 1 tablespoon of the olive oil in a blender or nourishment processor on high until smooth.
4. Shower or coat the bottoms and sides of the ramekins or preparing dishes with olive oil.
5. Include a spoonful of tomato sauce to the base of each.
6. Tear or cut the lasagna noodles into 4 pieces. Spot one bit of lasagna noodle, top with ricotta blend, top with a noodle, include sauce and mozzarella, and after that include the ricotta blend, and rehash.
7. For the last layer of each, top the majority of the ramekins with a lasagna noodle, a portion of the tomato sauce, at

that point a cut of the tomato and a sprinkle of the Parmesan cheddar and some crisply ground dark pepper.
8. Spread every ramekin firmly with foil and heat for 25 minutes. Evacuate the foil and prepare for an extra 5 minutes.

Nutrition Information: Calories 210g, Fat 14g, Carbs 9g, Sugars 4g, Protein 14g

Cauliflower Lasagna

Prep time: 45mins, Cooking Time: 55mins
Serving: 3, Smart Point: 5

Ingredients:

- 12 - oz. whole wheat lasagna noodles
- 1 - head raw cauliflower
- ¼ - pound white mushrooms
- 4 – cups milk
- ¼ - cup whole wheat flour
- 1 - large white onion, chopped
- 1 - tbsp. onion powder
- 2 - tbsp. olive oil
- 1- ¼ - cup grated parmesan cheese

Instructions:

1. Cook the pasta as coordinated. When cooked, channel and refill pot with virus water.
2. This will guard your noodles from staying together.
3. Saute the onion in 1 tbsp. Olive oil over low to medium warmth. Whenever finished, include the second tablespoon of olive oil and unexpectedly race in the flour.
4. Rush in the milk, a little at any given second, being certain to interrupt down any clusters from the flour with the whisk.

5. Try no longer to quit whisking considering the flour consumes within the container in all respects efficaciously, even after the milk is protected.
6. Include the onion powder and later on 1 degree of the cheddar.
7. In a gently oiled lasagna container, area the essential layer of noodles on the base.
8. Include a layer of cauliflower, at that point mushrooms and afterward sauce. Rehash.
9. Completion with noodles to finish the whole thing and after that sprinkle with the rest of the 1/4 field parmesan.
10. Spread delicately with foil and prepare at 350 stages F. For around 1 hour to at least one - 1/2 hours or until cauliflower is delicate and cooked via.

Nutrition Information: Calories 193g, Fat 8g, Carbs 27g, Sugars 8g, Protein 4g

❖ MORE HEALTHY WEIGHT WATCHER RECIPES ❖

Asian Chicken and Veggie Lettuce Wraps

Prep time: 1hr 25mins, Cooking Time: 55mins
Serving: 6, Smart Point: 7

Ingredients:

- 1 - pound skinless, boneless chicken breasts
- 2 - tablespoons canola oil
- ½ - red bell pepper
- 1 - inch knob ginger root
- 2 - garlic cloves
- 1 - carrot, peeled and sliced into thin strips

For the dressing:

- 2 - tablespoons sesame oil
- 1/3 - cup rice wine vinegar
- 2 - tablespoons lite soy sauce
- 1 - tablespoon of sesame seeds
- 1/16 - teaspoon cayenne pepper

For serving:

- 6 - large butter lettuce leaves
- 2 - green onions

Instructions:

1. In a medium bowl, whisk all in all the dressing fixings.
2. Add 1 tablespoon canola oil to an extensive sauté dish over medium warmth.
3. At the point when the oil is hot incorporate chicken strips.
4. Cook until the chook is super on all aspects and cooked by means of.
5. Add to the skillet extreme oil, carrots, pink pepper strips, and ginger.
6. Cook till veggies are basically imperceptibly fragile and still at the spotless angle.
7. Accumulate wraps by a method for putting down lettuce leaf, alongside the hen and veggies.
8. Top each wrap with diminishes unpracticed onions.

Nutrition Information: Calories 248g, Fat 15g, Carbs 10g, Sugars 5g, Protein 20g

Slow Cooker Pork Tenderloin

Prep time: 1hr 25mins, Cooking Time: 3hrs 55mins
Serving: 6, Smart Point: 6

Ingredients:

- 1.5 – 2 - pounds lean pork tenderloin

Marinade:

- 1 - cup chicken broth, fat-free, low-sodium
- 1 - tablespoon Dijon mustard
- 1 - tablespoon rice wine vinegar
- 1 - tablespoon liter soy sauce, low sodium
- 2 - tablespoons honey
- 2 - teaspoons freshly grated ginger
- 2 - cloves garlic, minced
- 1 - teaspoon curry powder
- ½ - teaspoon black pepper

- Kosher or sea salt to taste

Glaze:

- 2 - tablespoons honey
- 2 - tablespoons lite soy sauce
- 2 - tablespoons rice wine vinegar
- 2 - tablespoons ketchup
- 1 - tablespoon sesame oil
- 1 - tablespoon Dijon mustard

Instructions:

1. In a vast blending, bowl consolidates all marinade fixings. Trim away all obvious fat from tenderloin and dispose of.
2. Cut tenderloin into 2" pieces and spot in the marinade, guaranteeing all sides are covered.
3. Spread and enable tenderloin to marinate medium-term in the cooler.
4. Spot tenderloin and marinade in the moderate cooker, cook on low 4-6 hours on low, or until it shreds effectively with a fork.
5. Expel from the moderate cooker and spot on a serving platter.
6. To get a ready coating, add all fixings to a little pot, heat to the point of boiling, lessen warmth to a stew and cook around 5 minutes or until wanted thickness.
7. Pour coat over tenderloin.

Nutrition Information: Calories 252g, Fat 0.5g, Carbs 15g, Sugars 13g, Protein 32g

Slow Cooker Brown Rice and Chicken

Prep time: 1 10mins, Cooking Time: 2hrs 35mins
Serving: 8, Smart Point: 5

Ingredients:

For the Rice:

- 2 - cups organic Brown Rice
- 5 - cups water
- 1 14.5 -oz can organic ready cut diced tomatoes
- 4 - ribs organic celery
- ½ - large sweet white onion
- Sriracha hot chili sauce
- ½ -to 1 tsp cumin
- ½ - tsp paprika

For the Chicken:

- 4 - organic boneless/skinless chicken breasts
- ¼ to ½ - cup gourmet Yoshida sauce
- Sriracha hot chili sauce
- Heavy sprinkling of organic herb mix
- 1 - tbsp crushed red chili peppers
- 1 - tsp cumin
- 1 - tsp paprika
- ½ - tsp cayenne pepper
- 2 - fresh rosemary sprigs

Instructions:

1. In the event that you have two moderate cookers, cooking the darker rice and chicken in independent pots is perfect so they are done at near a similar time. Be that as it may, cooking independently and putting the rice in a bowl to keep warm while the chicken cooks are okay. Make the most of my Stay Healthy Slow Cooker Brown Rice and Chicken.

2. The key to this remarkable "constantly soggy" darker rice is the additional celery to the fixings. I have crocked a few

groups of darker rice and this is the best formula up until now and without fail. The surface of the rice is damp, never dry, notwithstanding while putting the scraps in the cooler for the week. The additional veggies and flavors make this rice delectable without having to extra fixings or zest. I like to side my rice with slow cooker chicken or flame broiled fish. Get your moderate cooker for a just sound and delicious side of dark colored rice.

3. In a Round 4-quart moderate cooker set to high. Stir the fixings in the vessel, put the top on and let it cook. Mix again around 2 hours in and to mind the rice. Continue cooking until all the rice is consumed and the blend is thick yet not soft.

4. Set a huge oval simmering pot to 6-hour cook, or the time you might want to have the chicken done. Utilizing a fork, move and coat all the chicken bosoms with the blend until equally joined. Spread and let the chicken cook for the distributed time chose. Open the cover and fork the chicken to shred and consolidate the juices and chicken together, until all is assimilated. Evacuate the rosemary sprigs and dispose of.

Nutrition Information: Calories 279g, Fat 3.4g, Carbs 40.5g, Sugars 2.1g, Protein 20.8g

GRILLED SALMON & ASPARAGUS GRATED EGG, BALSAMIC DRESSING

Prep time: 1hr 20mins, Cooking Time: 25mins
Serving: 4, Smart point: 5

Ingredients:

- 1 - egg
- 6 - asparagus spears
- 1 - pound salmon fillet
- ½ - teaspoon salt
- 2 - tablespoons extra-virgin olive oil
- 1 - tablespoon balsamic vinegar

Instructions:

1. Over medium-high warmth, in a pot with bubbling water, cooks the egg for around 7 minutes.
2. At the point when it's cooked and has chilled off, strip and put aside.
3. Over medium-high warmth, on a dry frying pan, flame broils the asparagus until they are cooked through.
4. When they have chilled off, cleave and put aside.
5. In a little bowl, blend half of the salt, the balsamic vinegar, and the additional virgin olive oil.

6. Shower them with the additional virgin olive oil and sprinkle with a large portion of the salt. Put aside.
7. In the equivalent hot frying pan, cook the salmon with the skin side down.
8. When you see that the fish is concocting midway, turn it over and cook the opposite side.
9. Mesh the hard-bubbled egg to finish everything.

Nutrition Information: Calories 246g, Fat 14g, Carbs 2g, Sugars 1g, Protein 28g

German Schnitzel, Slow Cooker Style

Prep time: 50mins, Cooking Time: 2hrs 25mins
Serving: 4, Smart Point: 11

Ingredients:

- 2 - butterfly pork chops
- 1 - egg white
- 1 - cup low fat buttermilk
- 1 ½ - cups whole wheat crumbs
- 2 - teaspoons black pepper
- Kosher or sea salt to taste
- 1 - teaspoon garlic powder
- 1 - teaspoon Hungarian paprika

Instructions:

1. Trim any noticeable fat from cleaves and cut each down the inside, the long way on the crease.
2. In a medium bowl consolidate crunchy bread morsels, 1 teaspoon dark pepper, 1/2 teaspoon garlic powder and 1/2 teaspoon paprika.

3. Whisk together egg, buttermilk, salt, 1 teaspoon dark pepper, 1/2 teaspoon paprika, and 1/2 teaspoon garlic powder.
4. Add pork to egg blend, spread, and place in the icebox and marinate for 60mins.
5. Spread bread pieces on a treated sheet. Expel slashes from egg blend, enable abundance to dribble off, add to bread morsels and thoroughly coat the two sides. Delicately splash the base and lower sides of the moderate cooker with nonstick cooking shower.
6. Likewise, daintily shower the two sides of pork cleaves with a cooking splash. Tip: We utilize a Misto olive oil sprayer.
7. On the off chance that a rack is accessible, place in the moderate cooker and organizes cleaves to finish everything, or place straightforwardly in the moderate cooker if a rack isn't accessible. Spread, cook on high 3 hours or low 6 hours on low, or until pork is cooked through and achieves an interior temperature of 145 degrees. There is no compelling reason to turn Schnitzel amid cooking time.
8. You can discover gluten-free Panko style bread pieces here.

Nutrition Information: Calories 409g, Fat 11g, Carbs 52g, Sugars 3g, Protein 30g

Quinoa "Meatballs" | Vegetarian Meatball Recipe

Prep time: 45mins, Cooking Time: 1hr 15mins
Serving: 6, Smart Point: 5

Ingredients:

- ½ - cup dry quinoa, pre-rinsed
- 1 - cup water
- 1 - cup cooked green lentils
- ¼ - cup diced red bell pepper
- ½ - cup diced onion
- 2 - cloves garlic, minced
- ½ - cup gluten free bread crumbs
- ¼ - cup freshly grated parmesan
- 1 - tablespoon flat parsley leaves
- 1 - tablespoon freshly chopped oregano
- ½ - teaspoon freshly ground black pepper
- Sea salt to taste
- ¼ - teaspoon cayenne pepper
- 1 - egg white
- 3 - tablespoons olive oil

Instructions:

1. Include pre-washed quinoa and water to a medium pot, unfold, warmth to the point of boiling.
2. Decrease warmth to a stew and hold cooking 15mins or until water is completely assimilated. Meanwhile, in an expansive non-stick skillet consist of 1 tablespoon olive oil, warmth to medium-low and sauté diced onions and ringer pepper till delicate round 4 minutes, consist of garlic, parsley, and oregano and sauté one greater second.
3. Expel quinoa from the warm temperature and permit to rest 10mins. Press down on quinoa with a paper towel to evacuate any high-quality water.

4. In an in depth mixing, bowl joins sautéed onion, garlic, parsley and oregano along outstanding fixings, with the exception of oil.
5. Use both a potato masher or fork and pound the fixings till the lentils are very an awful lot overwhelmed.
6. Utilizing your fingers, shape into 1 ½ "meatballs, location in a sizeable bowl, spread and refrigerate until chilled, around 2 hours.
7. Add remaining 2 tablespoons oil to a big non-stick skillet, warmth to medium-low and include quinoa meatballs.
8. Dark colored meatballs turn over and darker on the opposite side. Cook until seared and warmed thru around 16mins.
9. On the off hazard that you intend to serve these meatballs with marinara, add to the marinara sauce, tenderly swing to coat.
10. Stew until hot and serve over pasta.
11. These are best sustenance to consume earlier than working out as they deliver complicated starches to energy and protein for structure muscle tissue.
12. At the point when nearby, I'll have a couple before an exercise.

Nutrition Information: Calories 240.4g, Fat 8g, Carbs 27.4g, Sugars 0.1g, Protein 16.5g

Chicken Tikka Masala Pizza

Time: Prep time: 55mins, Cooking Time: 46mins
Serving: 2, Smart Point: 14

Ingredients:

Pizza Topping:

- 1 - lb chicken thighs, skinless and boneless
- 2 - cup strained tomatoes, or tomato sauce
- ½ - yellow onion, chopped
- 2 - garlic cloves, minced
- 2½ - tablespoons garam masala powder
- 1 - teaspoon dried ginger
- ½ - teaspoon paprika
- 1 - teaspoon salt
- pinch of cayenne pepper
- ½ - cup cashew cream
- 1 - cup smoked gouda cheese
- ½ - cup fresh cilantro

Crust:

- 1½ - cups whole raw cashews
- ½ - cup coconut flour
- ¼ - cup + 2 tablespoons almond flour
- 2 - teaspoons curry powder

- ➢ 1 - teaspoon baking soda
- ➢ ¾ - teaspoon salt
- ➢ 4 - eggs
- ➢ 1/3 - cup extra-virgin olive oil
- ➢ ½ - cup almond milk
- ➢ 2 - tablespoons cold water
- ➢ 1 - teaspoon apple cider vinegar
- ➢ (yields 2 9-inch pizzas)

Instructions:

1. Blend the tomato sauce, onions, garlic, garam masala, ginger, paprika, salt, and cayenne pepper and empty it into the supplement of a moderate cooker. Spot the hen over the sauce and cook on low for six hours.
2. At the factor whilst the sauce has half-hour left to cook, preheat your broiler to 350 tiers.
3. In a sustenance processor, granulate the cashews till a excellent flour has framed.
4. Include the almond flour, coconut flour, preparing the smooth drink, salt, and curry powder, at that point technique the blend for 1 minute.
5. Include the eggs, almond milk, apple juice vinegar, olive oil, and water and technique for one greater moment.
6. Rub down the edges of the bowl and heartbeat more than one more events till you have an incredibly easy batter.
7. Give the batter a danger to rest for 2 minutes to present the coconut a chance to flour assimilates a part of the fluid.
8. Sprinkle a bit of material paper with a touch almond flour, at that point flip the batter out onto the counter.
9. Sprinkle extremely more flour on the best factor of the bite of the aggregate, at that point place another little bit of fabric to finish the entirety.
10. Utilize your hands to stage the ball into a plate, at that point lightly reveal the batter into a circle this is 1/four inch thick.

11. Cautiously expel the great bit of cloth. You can also want to tenderly pull from the nook to get the fabric to discharge as it's far a sticky aggregate.
12. Slide the opposite piece with the out of doors layer onto a pizza dish. Prepare the hull for 12 minutes, or until it has overvalued quite and is wonderful dark colored around the edges. While the outside is heating, expel the fowl from the sauce and deliver it an ugly hack.
13. Expel the sauce from the warmth and mix within the cashew cream. Return the fowl returned to the sauce.
14. Brush the hull with a bit olive oil, at that point spoon the hen and sauce onto the pre-prepared pizza outsides, leaving a ½ outskirt of overlaying.
15. Sprinkle with cheddar, at that factor come lower back to the range and heat for a further 15mins till the cheddar has liquefied.
16. Appreciate

Nutrition Information: Calories 302.4g, Fat 14.5g, Carbs 19.4g, Sugars 5g, Protein 21.1g

Crustless Spinach Quiche with Sun-Dried Tomatoes

Prep time: 1hr 25mins, Cooking Time: 2hrs 46mins
Serving: 6, Smart point: 4

Ingredients:

Quiche:

- 6 - eggs
- 6 - egg whites
- 2 - cups loosely packed spinach
- ¼ - cup freshly grated parmesan cheese
- ½ - cup chopped sun-dried tomatoes with no liquid
- ½ - cup chopped onion

- 1 - clove garlic, minced
- 1 - tablespoon olive oil
- ¼ - teaspoon kosher or sea salt
- ¼ - teaspoon black pepper

Crust:

- ¾ - cups whole wheat pastry flour
- ¼ - cup oat flour
- ¼ - teaspoon kosher or sea salt
- 1/3 - cup coconut oil
- 2- 3 - tablespoons ice cold water
- 2 - tablespoons walnut pieces, optional

Instructions:

1. Preheat stove to 375 degrees.
2. Spot moved oats in a nourishment processor or blender and heartbeat until a coarse flour is made.
3. Combine the oat flour with the entire wheat flour and salt. Include the coconut oil in little pieces at once.
4. Mix with a cake shaper or hands or heartbeat in the nourishment processor until pea-like disintegrates is in the outside layer. Include the water in little sums until mixture is the correct consistency: Dough ought to be really shaggy and dry however met up when squeezed between the index finger and thumb.
5. Structure the batter into a ball. Wrap firmly in cling wrap and refrigerate for 30 minutes and as long as 24 hours.
6. Try not to stress if the batter is shaggy, it will meet up progressively after refrigeration. Move batter out onto a floured work surface. Spot the quiche/pie dish over the mixture, topsy turvy, and cut a circle. Cautiously transform over and press the batter into the pie dish and trim the edges.

7. Utilize a fork to create the external edges of the outside layer or use fingers and overlap over edges. Include the quiche blend (formula beneath).
8. Warmth onion and garlic in a skillet with olive oil for around 5 minutes, until onion is diminished and translucent. Include spinach and cook, just until withered. Expel from warmth. Blend in sun-dried tomatoes.
9. In the meantime, beat/whisk egg whites until foamy. Whisk entire eggs in a different bowl. Join the eggs and whites. Include parmesan cheddar, salt, and pepper. Overlap in the spinach tomato blend and fill the pie shell. Prepare for 25 minutes or until set in the middle and brilliant at the edges.
10. Whenever wanted, sprinkle with walnut pieces 5 minutes before expelling from the broiler.

Nutrition Information: Calories 131g, Fat 8g, Carbs 5g, Sugar 2g, Protein 10g

Slow Cooker Red Lentil Curry

Prep time: 50mins, Cooking Time: 2hrs 15mins
Serving: 8-10, Smart Point: 6

Ingredients:

- 2 - cups red lentils
- 1 - onion
- 1 - clove garlic
- 1 - tsp ground ginger
- ½ - tsp cumin
- 3 - tablespoons red curry paste
- 2 - tsp garam masala
- ½ - teaspoon turmeric
- 25 - oz. tomatoes pureed
- 1 - teaspoon salt
- 1/8 - ¼ - cup coconut milk
- top with green onions
- Garam Masala
- ½ - tsp Coriander
- ¼ - tsp Cardamom
- ½ - tsp Black Pepper
- ¼ - tsp Cinnamon
- ¼ - tsp Cloves
- ¼ - tsp Nutmeg

Instructions:

1. Wash the lentils and remove any horrendous ones.
2. To your mellow cooker, comprehensive of the onions, garlic, ginger, cumin, curry stick, garam masala, and turmeric.
3. Pour tomatoes over the lentil blend in the stewing pot. Refill the can with water and transfer to the mellow cooker.
4. Spread and cook supper on low for six hours until the lentils are delicate. Add salt to taste and coconut milk only sooner than serving.
5. At whatever point needed, serve Red Lentil Curry over a sleeping cushion of dull shaded rice or quinoa.
6. Top with fresh mint.

Nutrition Information: Calories 199g, Fat 2.9g, Carbs 31.4g, Sugars 3.5g, Protein 12g

Easy 20 Minute Chili

Prep Time: 5mins, Cook Time: 15mins
Serving: 6, Smart Point: 7

Ingredients:

- 1 - lb lean ground beef
- 1 - small onion, chopped

- 1 - clove garlic, minced
- 1 ½ - cup water or beef stock
- 1 - tbsp chili powder
- 1 - tsp salt
- 16 – oz. canned chili beans
- 6 - oz can tomato paste

Instructions:

1. Cook Meat, onion, and garlic in an extensive pan on medium-high warmth until caramelized, mixing to disintegrate the meat well.
2. Channel in a colander and flush with high temp water, come back to the dish.
3. Mix in water and remaining fixings.
4. Spread, lessen warmth, and stew 15 minutes, mixing incidentally.

Nutritional Information: Calories 278g, Fat 8g, Carbs 28g, Sugars 4g, Protein 24g

Conclusion

If you enjoyed this book, would you be kind enough to share this book with your family, friends, and or co-workers and leave a review on Amazon. By you leaving an honest review for this book on Amazon you will help guide people on Amazon to know that this book is legit and perhaps it can help them out as well.

Thank you for downloading this book!

Sincerely,

Andrea Zietlow

7/2019

CPSIA information can be obtained
at www.ICGtesting.com
Printed in the USA
LVHW112331060619
620481LV00001B/214/P